AF540836

UNIVERSITIES AND EXTENSION SERVICES

(FUTURE DIRECTIONS)

UNIVERSITIES
AND
EXTENSION SERVICES
(FUTURE DIRECTIONS)

By

Dr. P. Adinarayana Reddy

&

Dr. K. Sudha Rani

Department of Adult & Continuing Education
Sri Venkateswara University
Tirupati–517 502

DISCOVERY PUBLISHING HOUSE
NEW DELHI-110002

First Published-2006

ISBN 81-8356-138-1

Published by

DISCOVERY PUBLISHING HOUSE
4831/24, Ansari Road, Prahlad Street,
Darya Ganj, New Delhi-110002 (India)
Phone: 23279245 • Fax: 91-11-23253475
E-mail:dphtemp@indiatimes.com

Printed at:
Amit Enterprises

Preface

A university is a centre for the generation, advancement and utilization of knowledge, skill and attitude through scholarship, research and service. It is dynamic instrument of change in a society and as such it is bound consciously and constructively to relate its activities to national development by being responsible to national and specific community needs. In addition to the traditional academic programmes geared to the development of high level manpower to serve the growing nation and the discovery or creation of better ways of doing things, the institution must extended to the outside community. Every university should seek to identify public problems and needs, to interpret these concerns and to focus the university's skills and resources upon them. In essence, the outreach mission is to bring the campus and the community into fruitful juxta position thereby immeasurably enriching the activities of both. A university is obliged to step out into the main currents of life, actively seeking among the people to discover and define their problems. These problems, in turn inspire campus research.

In order to facilitate a systematic and sound approach to the integrated community development the expertise and academic talents of all the departments in the universities is very essential, because the task of integrated development is a multi-faceted one which requires multi-disciplinary approach. At present, extension has been treated as an area of practice of the only few departments of the university and confined to the departments like adult education, population education, sociology, social work and home science. Unless the involvement of all the departments, the third dimension of the university will become an exercise in futility. Hence, there is an urgent need to introspect the present status of the involvement of the university departments and to evolve the future directions to strengthen the university extension activities and to match the university expertise and the community needs.

In view of the above, an attempt has been made in this direction to compile the papers presented at the national seminar on **Universities and Extension Services (*Future Directions*)** by the academicians of different universities in order to know the present status of university extension activities, problems encountered and suggestions for the involvement of universities in the extension activities effectively. Finally, the editors expresses their gratitude to all the contributors.

Authors

Contents

List of Contributors

1. **Dr. N. Venkataiah**, Former Professor, Head and Dean, Faculty of Education, University of Mysore, Mysore–570 006, 11-246, S.V. Nagar, Tirupati–517 502.
2. **Dr. N.V.R. Kapali**, Director and Head, Department of Adult and Continuing Education, University of Madras, Chennai–5.
3. **Dr. A.S. Seetharamu**, Professor of Education, Institute for Social and Economic Change, Nagarabhavi P.O. Bangalore–560 072, India.
4. **Dr. S. Karuppaiyan**, Sr. Project Officer/Lecturer, Centre for Adult, Continuing Education and Extension, Bharathidasan University, Kajamalai Campus, Tiruchirappalli—620 023, Tamil Nadu.
5. **Dr. B.S. Vasudeva Rao**, Associate Professor and **Mr. P. Viswanadha Gupta**, Research Scholar, Department of Adult and Continuing Education, Andhra University, Visakhapatnam.
6. **Dr. G.V.R.R Prasad,** Dy. Director (Retd.) Directorate of Adult Education, Hyderabad.
7. **Dr. S.C. Jhansi**, Director, **Dr. Santosh Kumar Mishra**, Technical Assistant, Population Education Resource Centre, Department of Continuing and Adult Education and Extension Work, S.N.D.T. Women's University, 1, Nathibai Thackersey Road, Mumbai—400 020 (India).
8. **J.P. Dubey**, Sr. Project Officer/Sr. Lecturer, Department of Continuing and Adult Education and Extension, University of Delhi, Delhi—110 007.

9. **Dr. Bhalba Vibhute**, Director, Department of Adult and Continuing Education, Shivaji University, Kolhapur-416 004.

10. **Dr. N. Jayakumar Rao**, AMG India International, 50-44-4, Seethamadhara, Visakhapatnam–13.

11. **Dr. G. Lokanadha Reddy**, Prof. and Head, **Ms. K. Mythily**, Research Associate, Department of Education, Periyar University, Salem–11.

12. **Dr. M.C. Reddeppa Reddy**, Director, Department of Adult and Continuing Education, Sri Venkateswara University, Tirupati–517 502.

13. **Dr. T. Kumaraswamy**, Assistant Director, **G. Hussain Reddy**, and **Dr. K.G. Bharathi**, Project Assistants, Department of Adult and Continuing Education, Sri Venkateswara University, Tirupati–517 502.

14. **Dr. K. Rathnaiah**, Professor, **M.R. Gowramma**, Research Scholar, Department of Sociology, **Dr. R. Sampoornam**, Project Assistant Department of Adult Education, Sri Venkateswara University, Tirupati.

15. **Dr. K. Sudha Rani**, Associate Professor, Department of Adult Education, S.V. University, Tirupati.

16. **Dr. V. Reghu**, Assistant Director, Centre for Adult Continuing Education and Extension (CACEE) University of Kerala (P.O. Vikas Bhavan) Trivandrum–03.

17. **Dr. P. Adinarayana Reddy**, Director and Head, **Dr. D. Uma Devi**, Research Associate, Department of Adult and Continuing Education, Sri Venkateswara University, Tirupati–517 502.

18. **Dr. D. Janardhana Reddy**, Director, Department of Adult and Continuing Education, Sri Venkateswara University, Tirupati–517 502.

19. **Dr. Naseem Akthar**, Assistant Director, **Dr. K.K. Palani**, Research Scholar, Department of Adult and Continuing Education, Madras University, Chennai.

20. **Dr. P. Syama Thrimurthy**, Assistant Director and Head, Department of Adult and Continuing Education and Extension, Nagarjuna University, Guntur.

21. **Dr. H.M. Panchaksharaiah**, Professor and Chairman, Department of Social Work, Janasayahadri, Kuvempu University, Shankaraghatta–577 415, Karnataka.

22. **Dr. K. Parthasarathy**, Professor and Head, School of Education, **S. Durga**, Research Assistant, MSJE Project, Centre for Adult Continuing Education and Extension, Bharathidasan University, Tiruchirapalli–620 023.

1

Extension as Third Dimension of the University

Present Status, Problems and Future Directions

N. Venkataiah

What is Extension Education?

Extension education combines the adult education and also informal education. In it we are concerned with educating the adult farmers or home makers not in letters and alphabets, grammar or language but in the techniques of raising better crops, raising better animals, better fruit trees, managing home in a better way, rearing children scientifically, taking care of the nutrition of the family etc. With the area of our concern, we can call it as: (a) Agricultural Extension, when we extend knowledge to the agriculturists; (b) Veterinary and Animal Husbandry Extension, if we extend knowledge about breeding, managing, feeding and care of animals and birds etc.; (c) Agricultural Engineering Extension, when we extend knowledge about agricultural machinery—like tractors, pumps, levelling land, water use, soil conservation etc.; (d) Home Science Extension, when we extend the technical knowledge to farm wives, or ladies on foods, child care, home decoration, kitchen garden; (e) Industry Extension—when we extend knowledge on managing running industries.

Extension is formal and informal education aimed at assisting rural and even urban people to bring about continuous improvement in their physical, economic and social well-being through individual and co-operative efforts. It makes available to the villagers as well as to urban people, scientific and other factual information and training and guidance in the application of such information to the solution of problems in the concerned area and all sides of their life. University extension means extending knowledge from its faculty to the community, rural or urban on various subjects.

Extension As Third Dimension of the University—Justification

No University would justify its existence if it ignores the demands of the community in which it is situated and to which it owes its existence. It is essential that every University is a great seat of learning in the community should shoulder the responsibility of using the talents of the members of the faculties freely to all the members of the community who sincerely desire to get the benefits from the Universities. Formal education which is regular and full time expects a previous general education among the students for their admission. The work in the extension programmes is part time. These programmes need not require the previous formal academic training on the part of the participants. Maturity of mind, and a better grip of reality because of the experience of the world compensate for the lack of a previous literary training.

Gone are the days when the Universities remained isolated from the society as ivory towers. Today, in the Universities all over the world, in addition to teaching and research, third dimension namely, the function of extension has been accepted as legitimate work. It is well realised that it is only through the function of extension, the Universities can discharge their social obligation to the community. Almost all the Universities in advanced countries have realised the value of extension education programmes of one kind or another. Of late, Indian Universities too have started accepting the obligation that they should share new knowledge and technology with the surrounding communities for mutual benefits on both sides. In pursuance of this view, extension education programmes of different universities cater to the needs and problems of the community they serve.

The idea underlying in all extension programmes is that education is continuous process, that is not to be equated with studying for a degree does not cease with taking of a degree. Any extension education programme serves to impart vocational skills which may enable the person to improve his position in life, seeking his desire for knowledge or make him a cultural citizen without his having been an alumnus of a University.

Acceptance of extension work as a third dimension of the Universities is no doubt an ideal and welcoming future. But mere acceptance and implementation of extension programme will not alleviate the appealing conditions of the community. Such programmes, which could meet the needs and problems of the target groups should be planned pragmatically. Commitment and conviction towards social service and optimistic and liberal outlook are pre-requisites on the part of the organisers of the extension programmes. Step-motherly attitude or half-hearted attempt on the part of the planners of the extension programmes will kill the very purpose of extension programmes.

Extension education which has gained public support is envisaged as an instrument of social change. The National Policy of Education (1986) and the Kothari Commission (1966) have stressed the need of linkages of education with the society.

The Extension Programmes of the Universities will fall into two broad categories.

I. *Extension Services to Schools and Colleges:* The extension programmes of the University should help the schools to improve standards by inservice education of teachers, sharing facilities, provision of enrichment programme for students and discovery and cultivation of talent.

II. *Extension Services to the Community:* It should be the obligation of the teaching community to give extension lectures to interpret recent trends in their fields to the community, to create scientific awareness, to participate in adult education and workers' education programme etc. Universities can also help in the preparation of developmental projects for the community around them.

The extension activities bring about contacts between teachers in the Universities and citizens outside the University camps belonging to all walks of life especially those who have to earn their daily bread by the sweat of their brow and at the same time crave for an intellectual life which circumstances may have denied to them in their youth.

At present the extension activities are being taken up now and then by individual departments and they are not able to do much because they can not divert their attention completely to this programme. It is true that the efforts of the different departments events in the same University are not coordinated and hence there is no systematic and organised effort to fulfil the obligation of the University extension to the community. But the Home Science Department, Education Department, Population Education Centre, Social Work Department and Adult Continuing Education and Extension have been conducting extension programmes in a praiseworthy manner. Though the efforts of other departments are sporadic, the department/centre of Adult, Continuing Education and Extension is the only Department or Centre which has been doing yeoman service for extension work 90 to 95 per cent of extension programmes in a University are being attended by the Department/Centre of Adult, Continuing Education and Extension.

Objectives of Extension Education

The main objectives of extension programmes of the Universities according to the UGC are:

1. To enable the Universities to establish the necessary linkage with the community by offering need-based and relevant educational programmes;
2. To provide opportunities for disseminating knowledge in all walks of life in different segments of population for their intellectual growth, professional and technical competence;

3. To create to the felt needs of all people but specially to the needs of the less privileged and under-privileged sections;
4. To enrich higher education by integrating continuing and adult education programmes and extension work;
5. To provide an opportunity to the faculty and the students to an extension of field experiences—problems and realities; and
6. To enable the faculty and students participation in extension research and action research.

The Universities especially the Department/Centre of Adult, Continuing Education and Extension has an obligation to achieve these objectives.

I. State of Extension Programmes

a. Adult Education Programmes

When we say adult extension in the context of University, we mean all-round education for adults that would help for the development of personality and of wise and public spirited citizenship.

The Universities have come forward with three main purposes to be served through their adult education programmes. Firstly those programmes should provide development of vocational skills and better professional adjustment. Secondly, adult education should respond to the personality needs of adults for communication with other people who are interested in the same thing. Through wider knowledge adult education has to help in the development of personality or in acquiring hobbies and avocations. Lastly adult education has to prepare adults for community actions.

The main objective of adult education programme in Universities should be to educate and mobilise the masses and to involve them meaningfully in national development. The programme should also strive to make all adults particularly in the age group 21-35 functionally literate and lay the greater emphasis on the non-formal education of youth. A massive progamme of motivating, enthusing adults, training voluntary workers and institutions in the production of the University will have to be developed.

b. Continuing Education Programmes

Continuing Education Programmes have gained strength in Indian Universities in the last three decades. Summer institutes, summer schools, summer courses, refresher courses organised by various departments of the Universities attract professionals to learn about new developments in the fields. Number of seminars, workshops held by the departments of the Universities enable the scholars and experts to come together and exchange their views and discuss the problems in their fields to become aware of new trends and development in their chosen professions. Another important development in the universities under continuing education programmes is the popularisation of correspondence courses. Thus the universities have vast scope to extend the continuing education programmes to the community.

The Universities may organise general education courses in humanities, social sciences and sciences to enable an average citizen to keep his knowledge up-to-date, to understand public issues and the significance of the progress in the economic, social and scientific fields. Professional courses, courses in human relations, leadership and management skills, programmes for workers' education, training of personnel, programmes for the rural community etc. are some other continuing education programmes on which the universities may focus their attention.

Extension Programmes

The meaning of the term University extension is to be understood in three ways:

1. The extension of the University to the whole community;
2. The extension of University education throughout the lifespan of an individual; and
3. Extension of what a university stands for to all the vital interests of life.

The role of university extension, that too in a democratic community is of vital significance. But such efforts on the part of the Universities in the name of extension lectures are sporadic and all the strata of the community are not able to get the benefit of such programmes. The Universities have to increase different varieties of extension programmes to cater to the needs of as many categories of people as possible.

II. Important Recent Extension Programmes of Departments/ Centres of Adult, Continuing Education and Extension

1. Important Activities

Departments/Centres of Adult, Continuing Education and Extension are involved in literacy, post-literacy, continuing education, science for the people, environmental education, population education, legal literacy and technology transfer by involving teachers, students and through them to the adjoining communities.

2. Major Areas of Operation

The following are the major areas of operation of the Departments/Centres:

1. Bringing closer interaction between formal and non-formal education and out of school learning processes.
2. Accepting the philosophy of continuing education as part of the total education programmes of the institution.
3. Enriching the learning process of faculty and students through exposure to community needs, problems and reaching out to socio-economic and cultural groups.
4. Making educational content relevant to the learners needs and giving feedback to the curriculum roforms based on such experiences and
5. Attending the following major issues:
    - Gender, human rights and consumer rights issues;

- — Family life, education drugs, population education and AIDS and
- — Increasing incomes and skills for entrepreneurship and self-employment through micro-credit programmes.

3. Adult Extension Education for Outside the University/College Staff

Adult, Extension Education have information, education and Communication on various groups for skill development, income generation and entrepreneurship development. The programmes and courses are developed for peer educators, parents, housewives, industrial workers and professionals. The courses are need-based and target specific.

4. Community Outreach Activities

Community outreach activities include adoption of the community and programmes for specific target groups, such as child-labour, women, street children, older people. The Panchayat Raj institutions, health centres and political and religious leaders are carefully involved in participatory outreach programmes. The local people involved in programme planning, management and extension.

5. Training/Orientation

The Departments/Centres of Adult, Continuing Education have been involved in training/orientation to teachers and students on various developmental themes. Population Education Resources Centres set up in 17 Departments of Adult, Continuing Education have provided maximum training/orientation to College Principles, Peer educators, NSS teachers and volunteers on population and development themes. There is a lot of demand for the extension service of the University from the community. A large number of people would like to get the benefit of the University extension education. The University resources—financial and human resources are limited. The universities are not in a position to enhance their financial resources except the amounts they get from the UGC for extension service. The community in general is not in a position to contribute to the financial and human resources of the University. Therefore, the extension service of the University has not grown as is expected. Further the quality, variety and usefulness of the extension work is sometimes doubtful. It may further be noted that all the Universities do not have the Departments of Adult, Continuing Education and Extension. Only one-third of the Universities have Departments of Adult, Continuing Education and Extension.

III. Problems Faced by the Extension Departments/Centres

1. Certain adverse views which may be branded as 'Orthodox' are prevailing in the Universities about the extension programmes. According to this orthodox view, the implementation of extension programmes lowers the dignity of the Universities and interferes with more important and legitimate work of advancing genuine scholarship and research. Some academicians are of the opinion that the universities have to dissipate their energies on these activities which do not really belong to them. They further caution that the falling standards in teaching and research will still deteriorate if the Universities shoulder the responsibility of the extension programmes. These traditional academicians also suspect that if the Universities get too much involved in community affairs, the ideal and pure academic atmosphere may suffer through the interference of the community leaders. They also doubt the experience of using the time and resources of highly trained skills of the University faculties for activities such as adult, continuing and extension programmes while other problems of improving the standards of teaching and research are awaiting their attention. All these arguments do not carry any weight and such arguments have no place in the present set-up of the modern Universities. The UGC accepted extension as the third dimension equal in status to teaching and research. Nearly 105 Universities in the country

are involved in National Adult Education Programme through their Departments/Centres of Adult, Continuing Education set up by the UGC.

2. It is worth noting some reasons for the failure of extension activities in the Universities. A person who has no deep conviction and knowledge of the extension activities may be kept in-charge of the programmes. Sometimes a third rate person who is a misfit in his area of specialization has to be elevated with political pressure and such person will find place in persons who are successful as academicians and command respect from other academicians and administrators should be preferred. The success of the extension programmes depends on the organisational ability, dynamism, initiative, knowledge and perseverance of the person incharge of the programmes. If a 'fit for nothing fellow' is incharge of the extension programmes, they will lose their value and become routine, mechanical and uninteresting.

3. No staff member who is good both in academic and administration lines agrees to shoulder the challenging task of extension work unless and otherwise the universities accord extension department the same status as that of teaching and research. Extension department should not be looked upon as something peripheral and it should be viewed as the integral part and function of the University.

4. A critical analysis of the programme has clearly shown that only such Departments/Centres are successful where good leadership, having sufficient experience in extension education, is available. Some Heads/Directors of Adult, Continuing Education and Extension are not good academic leader. Such centres with efficient leadership are not able to perform well. Unless the UGC identify persons having requisite leadership quality and experience and provide to

them proper incentives and representation at national level, they are likely to quit and join some other lubricative jobs.

5. Each university, in turn, should also identify good academic leaders from the Department of Adult, Continuing and Extension Education and provide to them all freedom to undertake necessary activities/ programmes in this area. Unfortunately, most of the Universities pay low attention to this centre/ department. As a result, academic staff—its Project Officer, Assistant Director and Director strive hard for their survival, as the University system does not accommodate non-vocational academic/teaching concept.

6. In the past few years, the Departments/Centres of Adult, Continuing and Extension Education have acquired considerable experience of continuing education, population education, literacy and post-literacy activities, and extension work. However, activities/programmes in these areas are not uniform in all Departments/Centres/ as these depend on the leader (Head of the Department) and the ground work covered to generate demand inside the University.

7. Nearly 10 to 12 universities have teaching and research programmes including courses on non-formal education and distance education. However, teaching and research programmes are not receiving attention of good number of students. By and large, course and research activities are for the survival of the institutions and the core staff (teaching/academic staff) attached to this.

8. Literacy and Post-literacy activities which are the major attractions of the University system have been phased out and the Government structure and National Literacy Mission have been catering to the needs of Total Literacy and Post-literacy

Programmes. Thus the Departments though they belong to the Universities have been working like Government Departments without having their own programmes as per the requirements of the community around.

9. Few Universities and few scholars have successfully linked the activities and their expertise with National Literacy Mission and other institutions dealing with the activities. Hardly there has been any homogenous pattern of involvement leading to networking and liaisoning.

10. Several institution-based divergent courses (science, sports, journalism, modern mathematics for parents and public interest litigation, etc.) have been initiated by universities and colleges for the University and outside target groups. Their success has to be evaluated objectively and other universities can follow these examples for their advantage and benefit.

11. There are several apex level bodies in the field of Adult, Continuing and Extension Education. While conducting the programmes/activities such institutions, governmental or non-governmental should collaborate with each other. The institutions such as Indian Adult Education Association, Population Foundation of India, Council for Social Development. National AIDS Control Organisations and such organisations at the State Levels should come together for various extension programmes.

12. The Adult, Continuing and Extension Education Departments in the Universities have neglected their legitimate work, though they are expected to attend the following work:

    (a) Designing and developing curriculum framework and learning materials for various types of continuing education programme;

(b) Preparing multi-media packages for short duration training courses;

(c) Organising orientation courses and training programmes for the resource persons; and

(d) Production of material suitable for the courses and for neo-literates.

13. Some of the Extension Departments/Centres of Adult, Continuing Education, in general are functioning in isolation without proper linkages inside the University and outside the University. The activities of such departments are meagre and they do not attract the community as much as they are expected. They confine with the academic activities like any teaching and research department.

14. Some Adult, Continuing, Extension Education Centres have very small number of staff members—Director, Assistant Director and a Project Officer. The expectations of the Community around are many. The centre cannot satisfy all the expectations because the funds, training materials and manpower are not shared in planning, implementation of the various activities/programmes at the institution level and at the community levels.

15. In some Universities, the administrators do not have a comprehensive understanding of the purpose for which the Departments/Centres of Adult, Continuing Education and Extension are established. Therefore, they utilise the services of the faculty for the University administration neglecting the legitimate work for which the faculty is required.

IV. Future Directions

1. The Department/Centre of Adult, Continuing Education and Extension should not and cannot function in isolation. The Department/Centre should link its activities/programmes with NSS, social work, women's development and Academic Staff College of

the University. The several lessons learnt in this regard clearly indicate that those who have integrated various agencies and organisations including governmental and non-governmental sectors, are successful in providing the results. The lessons learnt indicate that funds, training, materials and manpower all should be shared in planning and implementation of the various activities/programmes at the institutions level and at the community levels.

2. Medial plays vital role in projecting prospects of extension education. The success story of Delhi University Helpline Counselling Services clearly indicate that if media both print and audio-visual are properly sensitized, extension issues can be successfully undertaken through the University system.

3. Adolescent and youth counselling through University-based hotline services on adolescent sexuality, personal problems, career issues, HIV, AIDS and substance abuse are highly successful. The first initiative was taken by PERC at University of Delhi in 1995. Several Universities such as SNDP, Mumbai, Rajasthan, Lucknow, Kerala, Utkal, Madras and Poona have started providing hotline services. The first hand experiences and data collected indicate that youth-based counselling has been highly successful. Thus, this should not be limited to the few Universities, rather each University should take steps in this regard.

4. The Department/Centre of Adult, Continuing Education in Institutions of Higher learning have a very useful and practical role to play. They have genuine contributions to make both in the sphere of policy-making and implementation. The University should undertake evaluation research and documentation of TLCs, PLCs and CEPs. The University system can be more focused in environment building and motivation.

5. The University system need to involve large number of students, teachers and non-teaching staff in extension programmes through their participatory involvement.
6. Thirty years of the University experiences have demonstrated that the extension system has been institutionalised in higher education. However, the progress in the various Centres/Department varied sharply and there is no uniform pattern. The University system has by and large, yet to accommodate extension vis-à-vis teaching and research. The experience of few Universities and a few academic leaders of Extension Education has paved the way of extension to be adopted.
7. The manpower of the University system employed in extension education should get proper direction and meaningful collaboration with the various sectors such as governmental, non-governmental and private.
8. The local level bodies such as Panchayat Raj Institutions, Political Leaders, Women's activities and religious leaders should be meaningfully involved in advocacy, motivation and programme implementation.
9. By and large, research in extension education remained a neglected area under the University system. Therefore, there is a strong need to initiate collaborative researches by involving NGOs government sector and the private sector in further strengthening researches under the third dimension. The involvement of experts, practitioners, field out reach workers and University researchers is necessary in the extension research.
10. The University Executive Council should thoroughly discuss the role of the Department/Centre and Core staff including technical staff. Through a national level meet, UGC should identify collaborative

activities with various international agencies (UNFPA, UNDP, UNESCO, UNICEF and WHO) Union Ministries and Planning Commission (NLM, Social Justice, MHFW), Women and Child Development) Private Sector (FICCI, PHD Chamber of Commerce) and prominent NGOs (like PFI, IAEA and AIU). The meet at National level will be helpful in planning the activities/programmes, chalking out their implementation strategies and sharing resources, trained manpower, success stories and constraints in implementation.

11. Without dynamic leadership and systematic planning it is not possible to advance extension education at the University level. The Department/Centre should play the pivotal role inside the University to strengthen extension as one of the most important components of the University system.

REFERENCES

1. Adiseshaiah, Malcolm S., "Thoughts on Continuing Education—Status and Future Directions," *Indian Journal of Adult Education*, Vol. 42, No. 7-8, July-August, 1981, pp. 27-30.
2. Hansraj Pal, "Extension Programmes in Schools and Community", *Journal of Educational Research and Extension*, Vol. 14, No. 3, January 1978, pp. 166-68.
3. Janardhana Reddy, D. "Extension Service in Universities," *Indian Education*, Vol. XI, No. 7, Oct 1981, pp. 16-18.
4. Rajesh "University Departments/Centres of Adult, Continuing Education and Extension: Challenges and Opportunities", *Indian Journal of Adult Education*, Vol. 62, No. 2, April-June, 2001, pp. 27-31.
5. Rajesh "Extension Education—Challenges, Priorities, Lessons Learnt during 1980-2000". *Indian Journal of Adult Education,* Vol. 63, No. 3, July-September, 2002, pp. 20-27.
6. Sushila Mehta. "University Extension" in *Crisco of Indian Universities.* Mansukhani. G.S. (Ed.); New Delhi: Oxford and IBH Publishing Co., 1972, pp. 89-102.
7. Venkataiah, N. and Adinarayana Reddy, P. "Significance of Adult, Continuing Education Programmes in Universities, *Indian Journal of Adult Education*, Vol. 45, No. 3, March 1984, pp. 2-6.

2

Paradigm Shift in Extension and Field Outreach

N.V.R. Kapali

Introduction

As pronounced by our father of Nation Mahatma Gandhi, 'India is living in its village.' It is a face that the country's development is depending on the development of its people, specially the people living in the rural areas. Many work towards the goal of improving the living standards of the rural masses by various approaches. Every citizen of the country has a duty to his/her motherland for its development. The student community also has the responsibility of doing their best in the development process. The Colleges and Universities are functioning with the short term goal as bringing in change in the individual for his/her own improvement and at longer terms the development (or) the welfare of the country-men. This has been institutionalised through NSS, NYK, NCC Scouts etc., by practising the Extension methods such as Drama, Rally, Action Research, People's campaign, Completion, film shows, folk arts, Social awareness campaigns, Exposure visits, Advocacy programmes, Puppet show, Villupattu etc., we were able to reach the minds of the people in the community. But now we realise that we need have a shift in the whole scenario of these methods. The following are the reasons why we want a paradigm shift.

Development

Development has, traditionally, been viewed as economic progress and growth, measured in terms of increase in GNP and per capita income and so on. But it is to be also viewed in terms of human development, improved standard of living, better health facilities, qualitative education, caring for differently abled, orphans, aged women and children and others.

Extension

The broader objectives of practicing extension are for 'Lab to land' approach, with the focus on increasing participation of students and teachers, facilitate the Educational inputs gets strengthened with field realities, bringing in attitudinal change in student's approach thereby quality of higher education influencing the society, increase mutual trust, credibility, reverence and acceptance to higher education and institutions, to bridge the gap between society and higher education.

The Clientele

Illiterates, Semi-literates, Neo-literates, Farmers, Agri-Labourers, SC/ST people, Backward classes, Leprosy patients, Social activists, Local body representatives, Unorganised labourers, School dropouts, Differently abled, Minority communities, Workers, Students, Teachers in colleges and Universities and others.

The Need for Paradigm Shift

- Most of the methods practised become cosmetic and failed to reach the minds of the rural masses.
- Human development through knowledge empowerment is the need of the hour.
- Modern trends of lifestyle.
- Development of Technology.
- To cope with the growing needs.
- To match with the trends of the people with whom we work.
- More on participatory mode, for better retention and feedback.

The PLM Approach

This can be described as a family of approaches, methods and behaviour that enable people to express and analyse the realities of their lives and conditions, to plan themselves what action to take, and to monitor and evaluate the results. Its methods have evolved from Rapid Rural Appraisal (RRA). The difference is that PLM emphasises processes which empower local people, whereas RRA is mainly seen as a means for outsiders to gather information. The terminology is confusing and there is much debate about what constitutes "real" PLM. The key elements of PLM are the methods used, and—most importantly—the behaviour and attitudes of those who facilitate it. Participatory learning and management (PLM) is an approach to the analysis of local problems and the formulation of tentative solutions with local stakeholders. It makes use of a wide range of visualisation methods for group-based analysis to deal with spatial and temporal aspects of social and environmental problems. It mainly deals with a community-level scale of analysis but is increasingly being used to help deal with higher level, systematic problems.

PLM grew out of a range of methodologies including agro-ecosystems analysis and rapid rural appraisal in the 1970s and 80s, in which the emphasis was placed on finding ways to express the diversity of local knowledge through facilitation by outsiders. It evolved from two distinct traditions: planners seeking to overcome the limitations of externally-dominated blueprint planning; and empowerment-oriented activists seeking to make their social transformation ideals more pragmatic. PLM is increasingly being used autonomously by communities but is now so diverse in application that it is hard to speak of a single methodology. The term is somewhat misleading because the combination of techniques are equally applicable in urban settings and are not limited to appraisal—they are linked to planning processes and are being adapted for monitoring and evaluation purposes.

PLM provides a structure and many practical ideas to help stimulate local participation in the creation and sharing of new insights. The emphasis on ensuring community feedback broadens the group of people involved. It is increasingly linked to participatory planning processes (e.g. using adapted forms of logical framework analysis). Although PRA was not intended to collect statistically significant information, it is increasingly used in combination with other methodologies to fulfil more scientific information needs and is easily made complementary.

There is no single way to 'do' PLM, although there are core principles and over 30 methods available to guide teamwork, do sampling, structure discussions and visualise analysis. The combination and sequence of methods will emerge from the context. Optimal ignorance and triangulation of findings guide the fieldwork in recognition of the need to know enough without knowing it all and to ensure that the qualitative insights are cross-checked by different sources using different methods.

Core Principles

- *Sustained learning process:* Enhancing cumulative learning for action by participants is the focus and has three outputs—identifying strategies for improvement, motivating people to undertake these strategies, and enhancing their capacity for solving problems;
- *Different perspectives in group-based analysis:* PLM explicitly seeks insights from and an understanding of the needs of different individuals and groups, which may be conflicting but will better show the complexity of local institutions;
- *Key role for facilitators:* To include different perspectives often means challenging local traditions of communication, which requires sensitive facilitation (often someone from outside the area but also increasingly a role taken on by someone with a local stake in the process);
- *Systemic and methodological basis:* Creating a structured process that explores problems within the wider context and not just focussing on a narrow slice of reality—from description to analysis and action; and

- *Context-specific:* Unique social/physical conditions means building a process of discussion, communication and conflict resolution which by necessity evolves out of the specific of the local context.

Methods

PLM employs a wide range of methods to enable people to express and share information, and to stimulate discussion and analysis. Many are visually based, involving local people in creating. The following are the methods or tools of PLM approach:

- Transect Walk
- Social Mapping
- Resource Mapping
- Vulnerability Mapping
- Opportunity Mapping
- Venn diagram
- Seasonal analysis
- Wealth ranking
- Participatory census method
- Mobility Map
- Family routine
- Historical trace
- Dream Map
- Cause-Effect diagram
- Force Field analysis
- Spider diagram
- Pair-wise ranking
- Livelihood analysis
- Time line
- Trends study and so on.

PLM activities usually take place in groups, working on the ground or on paper. The ground is more participatory, and helps empower those who are not literate. Visual techniques provide scope for creativity and encourage a frank exchange of views. They also allow crosschecking. Using a combinations of PLM methods a very detailed picture can be built up, one that express the complexity and diversity of local people's realities far better than conventional survey techniques such as questionnaires.

Behaviour and Attitudes

PLM depends on facilitators acting as convenors and catalysts, but without dominating the process. Many find this difficult. They must take time, show respect, be open and self-critical, and learn not to interrupt. They need to have confidence that local people, whether they are literate or not, women or men, rich or poor, are capable of carrying out their own analysis.

The Use and Abuse of PLM

Unfortunately, there has been much abuse of PLM by outsiders keen only to extract information quickly, and use it for their own purposes. Such practice is unethical because local people are brought into a process in which expectations are raised, and then frustrated, if no action or follow-up results. To avoid this, those wishing to use PLM methods in a purely extractive way need to transparent about their intentions, and refrain from calling what they do PLM.

In PLM, facilitators act as a catalyst, but it up to local people to decide what to do with the information and analysis they generate. Outsiders may choose to use PRA findings—for example, to influence policy or for research purposes. In all cases, however, there must be a commitment on the part of the facilitating organisation to do its best to support, if requested to do so, the actions that local people have decided on.

Advantages

The PLM has been practiced worldwide for its user friendliness and other flexible methods. The following are the advantages in practising the PLM method:

- Cost effective
- Required less time
- User friendly methods
- Consider all the sections of the people to get involved
- Allow us to get the first hand information from the people
- Chances for 'observation' during personal visits
- People are involved right from the planning stage
- Sense of ownership is built among the villagers
- The local people to take over the project

The Application

Since the early 1990s, PLM approaches and methods have evolved and spread with astonishing speed. Originating mainly among non-government organisations (NGOs) in East Africa and South Asia, they have since been adopted by government departments, training institutes, aid agencies, and universities all over the world. They are now being used in at least 100 countries, with PLM networks existing in over 30.

PLM has been applied in almost every domain of development and community action, both urban and rural. Examples include natural resources management, establishing land rights of indigenous people, slum development, HIV/AIDS awareness and action, anti-poverty programmes, disaster management, negotiation and conflict resolution, adult literacy and so on.

In the development process, participation of people is an important ingredient in the process of development. However, it is a missing link in most of the programmes. It is also experienced that if the user of the programme does not participate in planning, implementation becomes difficult and the sustainability cannot be ensured. One practical set of approaches, which was evolved and spread in early 1990s, bears the label of "Rapid Rural Appraisal" (RRA), then emerged as PLM, letter on PLM. This has been described as the best practical method to facilitate the benefactors to express, share and analyse their 'local wisdom' and to make decisions on different aspect for their good living.

The stake holder are the Local people, Community based organisations, Women and Children, Local youth, Local Body, Functionaries of the Government Departments, Local (informal) leaders, Activists, Representatives of the NGOs, Disadvantaged, Financial Institutions, Donors and others.

The Process

On the first day after the formal registration, importance to be given to the self-introduction games, which will create a good impact among the participants to know each other. This will also help in bringing their attention to the classroom situation. The self-introduction is insisted as the participants are drafted from different areas.

Experience Sharing Session

Since this is a participatory mode of programme, participants from various regions/districts come together and attend, and hence is always a scope of learning through others' experience. Hence a separate session is devoted for the experience sharing. This session is aimed at making a conducive environment for the participants to share their experience. This experience sharing session is a continuous process even at the hostels etc., where all the participants staying. As a result of these experiences sharing some of the participants get solutions to their problems of both personal and official. It is also useful in clarifying the doubts, based on other experiences.

- Collection of basic information on the Area
- Visit to the area in person
- Transect walk along with the people
- Discussions with people (experience sharing)
- Focused Group discussion
- Mapping exercise (through the process)
- Compilation of data

- Draft Village Development Plan
- Village meeting for data confirmation
- Execution of Plan in a phased manner
- Monitoring of Plan process
- Mid-term Evaluation
- Mid corrections in the plan
- Execution
- User Group Formation and Follow-up

Demonstrations

The demonstration on various Participatory Learning and Management technique tools also make significant change in the mindset of the participants by which their learning process is made easy, and as a result the level of involvement of all the participants in the training will be more. These demonstrations are done at the classroom situations and informally also.

Group Work

All the participants are made in to groups of 14 to 15, and one among them in nominated as the group co-ordinator. These groups are formed on the first day and the same group continued during the field works, home works and preparation of models, charts, diagrams, action plan preparation and presentations. Healthy competition among the groups made the members to perform better. Prizes are given away on the last day based on their performance on the parameters like the skills for involving the local people at the fieldwork, collection of data, time management, creativity in preparing the charts, action plan etc.

Field Visits

All the field visit exercises are done as a group setting. All the participants are made into two groups. Each of these groups is sent to habitations, mostly adjoining villages. All the two groups are made to practice all the field exercises right from warming up games to preparation of action plan after careful execution of the Participatory Learning and Management technique tools.

Warming up Games before Starting

All the field visit undertaken every day after the classroom sessions are to be started with warming up games to prepare the participants psychologically to undertake the field exercises such as visiting all the streets, meeting the households, arranging for the village meetings etc. These warming up games at the campus proved to be good in motivating the participants towards the task performance.

Ice-breaking Rapport Building Techniques

Similar to the ice-breaking done among the participants on the first day at Training Institute, ice-breaking exercises/ games are to be performed at the village, by the participants. Some of the ice-breaking games and rapport buildings techniques taught in the classroom are to be performed by the participants according to the field situation.

Fieldwork usually lasts for to ten days. The research techniques, questions and focus of the research may be amended as the research progresses. Frequent team meetings are held (perhaps once daily for the entire team, twice daily for sub-teams) to share material and insights; identify major patterns and relationships:

1. The community discusses and ranks its problems, to see where educational problems fit in—have they a high or low priority? Often separate group discussions are held—older/younger people; men/women; members of different religious or ethnic groups, castes, etc. Sometimes, cultural dictates require this; other times, the perspective of each group is so different that it may be lost in a large group discussion. If separate group meetings are held, the results have to be integrated eventually, and the concerns of each group negotiated with the others.
2. Then the group or groups discusses its specific educational problems, and its current coping strategies, and possible solutions. Girls' education is then focused upon. The problems and solutions are

drawn in a grid or matrix on the ground by local people—some problems might be school fees, fears for girls' security, distance from home, need for girls to work at home, etc. Some solutions might be a community savings scheme, help from NGOs, better marketing facilities, more female teachers, payment of fees after the harvest, expansion of a Koranic school, flexible schools hours, childcare facilities at the school, etc. Symbols, such as matchboxes, tins, leaves, are used to represent the various problems and solutions. This allows those who cannot read and write to participate.

The community then discusses how, for each problem, to allocate seeds, beads or other objects across the various solutions, with the best solutions for each problem receiving the most seeds. The result is a graphic display, easy to understand, of problems in order of importance, some possible solutions, and which solutions are thought to make the biggest contribution to each problem. Solutions which cover several of the most important problems may be strategies worth looking at further.

3. People draw a map of the community, indicating each household/compound, and the school-going age of children or each sex who are going/not going to school.
4. Using the information on the map, the team might list each household on a card. Working with a smaller group of six or seven, it asks people to sort the cards into meaningful categories. In this sample, project, we ask them to sort the cards by "well-being"—which households are comfortable and secure? We then try to relate the resulting piles to educational participation—for example, do the people in the "poor" category generally send all their children to school, or only some, and if so, are they boys or girls? The same is done with every category. The results can be compared with the map—household 22 is poor—does the card sort reflect what the map said?

This technique gives a lot of information, such as how local people group themselves, and what they think the groups do, but at this simplest, it acts as a check on the map. If they don't agree, more research is needed. (Sortings can also be made by ethnic group, religion, distance from school, education of parents, etc.)

5. The map can also be used to develop a sampling procedure for selecting households/individuals to interview. Selection may be *random* or *purposive* (i.e. typical cases, critical cases, contradictory cases, extreme cases, "information rich cases"). Individuals may also be interviewed at random, especially school-aged children, as a check to see if they appear on the map.

Interviews can take the form of simple questionnaires, semi-structured interviews, case-studies, etc. The team may want to collect information on the daily activities of girls, how poor families manage to send children to school, how "successful" women have managed to reach their goals, etc.

6. A variety of other techniques from the "basket" can be used now: for example, a calendar showing the months or seasons can be drawn on the ground and income, school expenses, demanding work periods for girls/boys, demanding school periods, etc. can be plotted. Do people have least income at the high points for school expenditure? Is girls' work heaviest at the most demanding times of the school year? People can also draw pie charts to show school expenses as a portion of total expenditure, or to show family income resource, or time allocation, etc.

7. The findings are then reviewed with the group(s). Corrections, additions, etc. are invited. Each group chooses 3-5 of the most serious problems which can be addressed largely through local resources, and identifies possible solutions. Once again, for those

who cannot read, symbols, pictures or cartoons can be used to remind people of the problems which have emerged during the research. Then, in a community-wide meeting, the results are pooled, and 3-5 common problems selected. If individual groups (for example, men and women) are unable to meet, the choices of each have to be conveyed to the others, perhaps by a team member, and some common problems have to be chosen.

8. Then consultations are held among the PRA team, representatives of the local community and any necessary experts who may be required to help work out several options for carrying out each of the possible solutions to the community's problems. Inputs, skills, costs, materials, are all worked out.

9. The various options for addressing each problem are assessed by the local people, through voting, ranking, or various other options assessment techniques in the PRA "basket". Emphasis is placed on choosing solutions which can be carried out and sustained mainly through community mobilization, with minimal external help, unless an appropriate external agency is involved in the process. Fairness, low cost, quicker results all inter into the voting considerations.

10. A community action plan is made, spelling out which options have been selected, how they will be carried out, what is to be done, input and output indicators, who will be responsible, how people will measure "success."

11. A community resource survey may be made, to determine the extent to which the community can mobilise itself to carry out the options selected. At the same time, village institutions, NGOs, international donor agencies, religious groups and government departments may also be ranked in terms of their possible role in contributing resources.

Limitations

- To take this method for execution in the field, some trained personnel required
- Each of the places to be visited in person, hence more number of personnel required
- The mindset of the local people is subject for fluctuation and hence, at most care to be taken for sustaining the decisions
- In the process of decision-making, there should be enough efforts for consoling the entire community
- Only recognised and practiced in NGO sector

Conclusion

It is seen from the above details that, through the other methods practiced in present has it merits and demerits, the advantages of following the Participatory Learning Methods are more and the method is very user friendly, and that is reason why, it has been accepted by the International community, and the UN organisations itself insist to follow this methodology in community development and other development projects as one of the compulsory parameters in the project planning and implementation. It is no doubt that the academics will use this approach in reaching even the unreachable to bring positive change in their living standards and finally empower them by all means.

TRAINING MODULE—DAYWISE TIME PLAN

Day: 1 (Fore Noon)

Registration - Warming up games - Pre-evaluation - Self-Introduction through games - Experience Sharing - Theory on the historical perspective of the participatory methods.

(After Noon)

Need, scope and concept of People's participation in Developmental process with special reference to the Nutrition and Health schemes.

Day: 2 (Fore Noon)

Reinforcement on the yesterday's programme—Introduction to the PLM techniques - Pre-requisites for PLM practitioners - 'Dos' and 'Don'ts' in PLM Application - tools to PLM Rapport building - Transect Walk - Village meeting Social Mapping - Resource Mapping - Time line.

(After Noon)

Field visit : Tool of PLM Application - Rapport building - Transect Walk—Village meeting—Social Mapping - Resource Mapping - Time line - Learning by doing - experiencing with the community.

Day: 3 (Fore Noon)

Reinforcement on the yesterday's programme and Field Visit - Case studies on the PLM application - Venn Diagram - Seasonal Calendar Focused Group Discussions.

(After Noon)

First visit : Tool of PLM Application - Venn diagram - Seasonal Calendar Focused Group Discussions - Learning by doing - Experiencing with the community.

Day: 4 (Fore Noon)

Reinforcement on the yesterday's programme and Field Visit - Wealth ranking—Matrix Ranking - Family daily routine - Problem cause analysis—Nutrition calendar - Learning by doing - Experiencing with the community.

(After Noon)

First visit : Tool of PLM Application - Wealth ranking - Matrix Ranking—Family daily routine - Problem cause analysis - Nutrition calendar - Learning by doing - Experiencing with the community.

Day: 5 (Fore Noon)

Field visit: Data conformation with the people Demonstration of all the charts/models made by the people and the participants on various tools of PLM like Transect Walk -

Village Meeting—Social Mapping - Resource Mapping - Time line - Venn Diagram - Seasonal Calendar—Focused Group Discussions - Wealth ranking - Matrix Ranking - Family daily routine - Problem cause analysis - Nutrition calendar and getting acceptance for the Action Plan - Learning by doing - Experiencing with the community.

(After Noon)

Presentation of the Group Reports - Charts and Models - Action Plan for the village - with special reference to the - Nutrition and Health—Post Evaluation and Course Feedback.

3

Higher Education for EFA

Fusion of Intellectualism with a Heart and a Soul

A.S. Seetharamu

This brief note on the space and role of higher education in promotion of EFA objectives is written with the assumption that the limited interest of Universities/Higher Education in EFA is due to the conceptual foundations of universities all over the world. It calls for a deliberate, sustained and concerted campaign to expose the false foundations of intellectualism of the universities directed towards individual FREEDOM with the use of Intellect and Reason and then onwards to move towards the qualities of Heart and Soul glorified by the values of JUSTICE and EQUALITY. The EFA movement symbolises the values of Justice and Equality which ultimately sets not only the individuals FREE but heralds Freedom for the entire humanity. This presentation is composed of the following sections:

- Intellectual Apathy to EFA in Historical Perspective
- Causes of Apathy
- Universities in EFA—Present Status
- Universities in EFA—The Future
- What can the Universities do?

Intellectual Apathy to EFA in Historical Perspective

The apathy of the intellectual community to mass education is proverbial. It is a fact of history that the first ever attempt to include mass education as an agenda of a political manifesto was by the 'Sans Culottes' who came to power in France in 1791, after the French Revolution. This was the first ever, short lived, common people's government.

Free public education expanded on a large scale in the United States only after the American Civil War.

Even in England, a Parliamentary resolution for mass education was adopted in 1881. It is to be noted further that both France and England have a history of university life on modern lines for over 800 years. As such, interest in mass education initially grew outside the university community life. The first ever 'normal' school proposed by the Frenchman Victor Cousin (1792-1867) for Massachusetts State, on the lines of seminaries of Prussia were set up outside the University Umbrella. [*Note:* the French word 'normal' is an equivalent of the English word 'model'. This was a school set up to train better quality teachers for elementary schools].

In fact, even by 1889, the University Community in the United States was divided on the issue of involvement of the universities in training of teachers. [John S. Bhubacher: "*A History of the Problems of Education*", McGraw Hill, 2nd Ed. New York, 1966]. Over a period of time, it was because of the interest evinced by a few great educationists connected with university life such as Stanley Hall (1846-1924), John Dewey (1859-1952) and Edward Lee Thorndike (1874-1949) that the universities began to take interest in elementary education through the training of teachers.

It needs to be noted that the universities got interested in continuing education of adults, not basic literacy programmes, as early as by the end of the 19th century. John Cardinal Newman (1801-1890) visualised three basic functions for the university: teaching, research and extension. The university tried to reach the larger community and transfer the profound knowledge of the physical, natural and social universe around us to the common people. This knowledge had been created through research in the universities. The extension services wing of the university achieved this task through organisation of lectures by scholars of distinction and achievement and by publishing these lectures in popular and simple language.

The interest of the university in school education is a post-second World War phenomenon. This is also associated with the democratization of the colleges and the universities. Otherwise, elitism fused with intellectualism regulated university functioning.

Even in India, down South, there is the case of the University of Mysore established in 1917, the fifth university established in the country and the first in the 20th century. It is a pity that the district in which the university is located ranked very low ($18^{th}/19^{th}$) on literacy rate ranking across the 20 districts of Karnataka State even by 2001 AD. This is a case of '*Shadow under the Lamp*'.

Causes of Apathy

Why is there apathy in universities for involvement in EFA?

There are several reasons for the apathy of the universities to universalisation of elementary education and adult literacy. Some of them are internal to the conceptual foundations of the university while others are external to it.

a. 'Intellectualism' of the universities is the major obstacle to involvement of universities in EFA. What is 'intellectualism'? 'Intellectualism' is a summary term for the following a priori belief: "The universe around is spiritual in essence. It is a great and grand IDEA. The discovery of the principles of functioning of the universe around us is the purpose of life. Knowledge and understanding which composes these principles is worthy of pursuit. Such knowledge liberates the mind from all bondages of life. Ignorance is bondage and knowledge is freedom. Freedom is the end-goal of life. Higher education liberates the mind. The universities are institutions where human beings use their intellect, reason and judgement, the highest faculties of the mind, to understand the dynamics of the universe around us. Universities are

> institutions of excellence, higher knowledge. The word university is from the root word 'universe'. Higher education means education for the pursuit of 'higher' order of knowledge of the universe. Knowledge of the material world in lower order of knowledge. The university dons have transcended this lower order and have to 'look up' for higher knowledge. It is the intellect, the rational power of the mind which helps in this pursuit. The human 'mind' itself is a 'MICRO-IDEA' and hence spiritual in essence. The intellect is the functional component of this micro-idea. Higher knowledge, knowledge pursued through a refined intellect is profound, scholarly, discipline-based and worthy of life. All other mundane, worldly knowledge and actions are useless and fit enough for people who are engaged in lowly occupations and who do not need to use their intellect for their livelihood."

Intellectualism is not limited to the universities and university/college teachers/researchers. It gets percolated into the system of public life through the products of universities who enter higher order of public life, the bureaucracy, scientific and technological research establishments, the literary world; media-print and electronic; the judiciary; and the world of medicine.

The poor, the downtrodden, the illiterates, the marginalised, the impoverished, the exploited and immiserised classes of people and their upliftment/liberation does not enter the styles of thinking and structure of intellect of the university and university-bred intellectuals. Efforts of microscopic minority of university bodies/teachers/administrations who get interested in community concerns such as EFA either because of their job-concerns or commitments appear quite profane for the intellectuals.

Hence, a new beginning for involvement of university in EFA has to be made with deliberate, systematic and concerted efforts for destroying the foundational beliefs of intellectualism. A global campaign is needed to redefine the functions of a university with supportive logic and logistics.

b. Another source of apathy of the universities to EFA stems from the poor quality of teacher training programmes. Let alone the hard-core departments of the universities, even the colleges of education/teacher training colleges at the B.Ed. level and P.G. Departments of Education, with honourable exceptions, are not aware of the problems and issues of elementary education and literacy. They have practically no interest in such concerns. Their involvement is very poor. Except the teacher educator who teaches a paper on 'Current Problems of Education,' the others identify themselves and their interests in a piece-meal fashion with the subjects they teach such as educational psychology, educational philosophy, educational sociology, educational planning and management, evaluation and test construction, special education, population education, women's education, etc. They have hardly any understandings or concerns regarding the scale and magnitude of EFA problems. This is true of training colleges which prepare teachers for elementary level of education. The colleges of education are normally affiliated to the universities. They focus mainly on secondary education.

c. Education has not attained the status of an independent discipline. It cannot be an independent discipline as Philosophy, Psychology, Sociology, Political Science and Statistics. Everyone knows that it is a cognate discipline. Even as a cognate discipline, it does not enjoy a status unlike those of Medicine and Law. Much of the knowledge-base in education today is a product of application of first principles of such disciplines as Psychology, Sociology, Economics, Public Administration and Statistics to understanding of educational problems. Knowledge flow is top-down. Research and production of knowledge about school education which is from the grassroots is needed. Currently, school experiences are hardly documented, shared and systematised to build bottom-up systems of knowledge. Universities can help in production of such knowledge systems with external funding support. John Dewey had observed that 'Educational Theory is a guide to Educational Practice and Educational Practice can serve as a corrective to Educational Theory." The second part of this proposition is still to become a complete reality. The intellectual tradition of the university looks down upon 'trial and error' knowledge system of 'EDUCATION'.

Universities in EFA—Present Status

It is incorrect to observe that universities are not doing anything of EFA. Something is being done which is far from adequate. Some of the activities that the universities in India are engaged in context of EFA since the 1950s are as follows:

The Universities Grants Commission (UGC) of the Government of India, autonomous in its functioning, has financed the setting up of separate Departments of Adult and Continuing Education in Universities of the Country. They are mostly into promotion of concerns of adult education through the affiliated colleges. They enjoy low status across University Departments.

The UGC had adopted villages in the 1980s to promote adult literacy through the running of centre-based adult education projects.

The UGC launched a Mass Programme of Functional Literacy (MPFL) in 1986 through the colleges of universities. The National Social Service (NSS) scheme of the UGC was used for this purpose. It was a voluntarism-based approach. However, many programmes of the UGC went on a low-key after the setting up of the National Literacy Mission Authority in India in 1988.

A research review of the MPFL in 1990-91 revealed that the programme had promise and potential. But it was given up.

The contribution of universities in India to elementary education is highly limited. This observation is made in the context of the size and magnitude of university education system in India. Academicians in their individuals capacity have assisted, facilitated the promotion of EFA goals. The response of the system as such is quite poor.

Universities in EFA—The Future

A New Conception

The conception of the university as an institution for liberation of the individual from all system of bondages should be exploded at the outset. A realistic conception would be as follows: "The university is a community institution set up by a community. It has to raise a community to higher heights of excellence and glory and promote universal values therein. It is a harbinger of refined culture of a community. It has the strength and potential to achieve this goal as it controls/ regulates/facilitates a large volume of student body/the privileged youth of a nation through its colleges and post-graduate departments. The university has to think globally and act locally."

The nursery for pursuit of excellence in university life are the elementary schools. The quality of elementary schools determines thereby the quality of intellectual pursuits at the university/research level. The university has to recognise this reality. Apart from other reasons which are noble, the university system has to take interest in elementary education of the nation in its own enlightened self-interest.

Justice and Equality are as noble, spiritual, eternal, permanent values of life as Liberty is. The university should promote Justice and Equality in society through its involvement with EFA. The concepts of Liberal Education, Liberal Arts Colleges, Liberation as a goal of education (SA VIDYA YA VIMUKTAYA – a Sanskrit rooted definition of higher education which means that 'education is that which liberates'; SHIKSHANA is equated with school education while Vidya is equated with Higher Education), should all be transplanted with the concepts of higher education as an institution for promotion of Justice and Equality too. In fact there can be no Freedom without Equality and no Equality without Justice in the contemporary inegalitarian and unjust world order. Promotion of Justice and Equality should not be confined to Protective Discrimination/Affirmative Action strategies. It should extend to the masses of population and not just confined to the elite among the poor and disadvantaged. Universities should disrobe themselves from the values of Intellectualism and put a new robe woven from the fabrics of Justice, Equality, Human Rights and Global Peace.

What can the Universities Do?

The main contribution of universities regarding EFA can be as follows: a short-run concern for universalisation of basic literacy in their respective regions which can mean adoption of a cluster of villages; a long-term concern for production of literature and in-service training for continuing education programmes; a long-term, stable concern for the provision of support systems to supply teachers of quality and excellence for elementary levels of education; production of literature/ extra-reading/referencing materials for teachers—Teacher Reference Books on syllabi that elementary teachers need to transact in their classroom contexts; training in action-research techniques of elementary teachers and elementary level educational administrators; faculty research on determinants of school quality, school effectiveness; learning attainments; managerial efficiency; stakeholders involvement in school management etc., fundamental research on learning, motivation, group processes, creativity, individual differences in behavioural and cognitive attributes and characteristics, etc., monitoring and supervision of macro-correlates of schooling; facilitation of planning and implementation of national/regional macro-projects; evaluation of school projects; and training in documentation of school processes, action research insights and publication of school magazines and newsletters.

4

Extension as Third Dimension of the University

Present Status, Problems and Future Directions

S. Karuppaiyan

In general the term 'Extension' originated in England in 1866 with a system of University Extension which was taken up first by Cambridge and Oxford Universities and later by other educational institutions in England and in other countries. The above term had been is use more than a century ago in the world. The term extension education was first used in 1873 by Cambridge University to describe this particular educational innovation. According to Ensmingar (1957) "Extension is education and that its purpose is to change attitudes and practices of the people with whom the work is done."

The National Commission on Agriculture (1976) states "Extension as an out-of-school education and services for the members of the farm family and others directly on indirectly engaged in farm production, to enable them adopt improved practices in production, management, conservation and markoting." According to Van den Ban and Hawkins (1988) the term 'Extension' involves the conscious use of communication of information to help people from sound opinions and make good decisions. Thus 'Extension' may be defined as the science of making people innovative for improvement in their quality of life. Extension, in addition to practicing in the field, is formally taught in colleges and universities leading to the award of degrees. Research is also carried out in extension. The uniqueness of extension is the applicable of the knowledge of this discipline in socio-economic information of the rural communities.

The fundamental objective of the extension is to develop the rural people economically, socially and culturally by means of education. In this context Swansen and Claar (1984) stated that the objective of university extension was to take the educational advantages of university to ordinary people. Under these circumstances, the concept of extension education is used in educating people about agriculture, industry, home science, dairy, veterinary, science or public health. It tries to bring out three types of changes in human behaviour through knowledge or things known, skills or things done and attitudes or things felt. Thus, extension education is a teaching and learning process and educational programme for the people, based on their needs and problems.

Extension as Third Dimension of the University

It was about five decades ago in 1960 that the Kothari Commission first articulated the concept Extension and the TRINITY of Teaching, Research and Extension. Accepting these recommendations, the University Grants Commission in their policy frame on Higher Education recognised Extension as the third dimension of the Institutions of Higher Education in addition to the earlier two-fold dimensions of Teaching and Research in the following words: "If the University system has to discharge adequately its responsibilities to the entire education system and to the society as a whole it must assume extension as a third important responsibility and give it the same status as research and teaching. This is a new and extremely significant area which should be developed on the basis of his high priority." The acceptance of Extension as the Third Dimension equal in importance to teach and research was in the context of a growing realization that Universities and colleges having institutional resources namely knowledge, manpower and physical have an obligation to develop sensitivities to involve the development of the community with particular reference to overall and diverse learning needs of all segments of the people of the community. The third dimension was to aim at promoting a meaningful and sustain rapport between the Universities and the community. Its objective, firstly, was to extend knowledge and other institutional resources to the community and vice-versa and secondly to gain insights from a contact between knowledge resources and social-cultural realities with a view to reflecting these in the entire curricular system of higher education including teaching and research.

Development Programmes under the Third Dimension under Aegis of UGC

Keeping the importance of Extension Dimension in view, the Government of India provided the first major opportunity by announcing the National Adult Education Programme (NAEP) in 1978 to involve Universities and colleges, through their students and teachers to provide education to those sections of the communities which were earlier denied access to such opportunities. In all 92 Universities and 2,138 colleges in 18 states and 2 Union Territories had been involved in this programme. Centres/Departments, for Adult and Continuing Education was set up in Universities. Thereafter the Adult Education Programme as point 16 of the 20-point programme of the Government of India was introduced (1983-1989) followed by Area Based Approach Programme (1989-1992) and the Total Literacy Campaign (1992-1997) of the National Literacy Mission.

In the Ninth Plan the UGC continued the Adult and Continuing Education Programme in a manner that facilitated the Centres/Department of Adult and Continuing Education and Extension to cast their own Plan of Action for the Extension Dimension specific to their own University. In all, the programmes introduced by the UGC from time to time, the main focus has been on Adult Literacy, Post-Literacy and Field Outreach Programmes. Attention was given in the Ninth Plan to Adult and Continuing Education for University groups. In the Ninth plan, the UGC has implemented the schemes under its Non-Formal Education Bureau. As evidenced from the UGC's vision and strategy for the X plan, the scheme will continue to be operationalised by UGC under their Non-Formal Education Bureau. In order to ensure continuity, the UGC has already released grants to departments for the years 2002-2003 and 2003-2004.Current scenario of extension dimension under × plan in university departments of adult, continuing education and extension. The guidelines (2004) issued by UGC for the Tenth Plan period clearly state all the activities such as Thrusts, Target groups, Programmes and Activities, Role and Functions of the Departments, Organisational aspects (status of the Departments of Adult and Continuing Education, Education, Extension Work and Field Outreach, Nomenclature, Structure, Faculty and Staff) Nodal Universities, Administrative and Financial procedures, Funding Criteria and pattern of assistance that Department of Adult and Continuing Education and Extension has to conduct/envisage during the X plan period.

Thrust Areas

The following are thrust areas to be focused under Extension and Field Outreach.

- Continuing Education Programmes at grassroot level through the CECs of the National Literacy Mission and through the National Institute of Open Schooling and State Open Schools;
- Communal harmony and peace education;
- Human rights and rights of vulnerable groups;
- Environmental issues;
- Health education for the community and through the healthcare centre of the University;
- Women's empowerment and social issues and gender issues;
- Initiating change in policies and procedures of the University so as to make the University courses more accessible to the adult learner; and

- Establishing a new relationship with government organisations, NGOs, Civil societies, NGO networks and other professional bodies to address social issues.

Target Groups

- Groups/Students in the colleges and University system;
- Groups who have passed out of University system and need to return for upgradation or the acquisition of new skills from industry and service sectors;
- Groups who are already in services or the underemployed or the unemployed who need to enhance that employability;
- Groups which would normally not be entrants into the University system; women, SC/ST disadvantaged street children, bonded labour, child workers etc;
- Neo-literates, CE learners, out of school youth; and
- Senior Citizens.

The extension activities under the Third dimension of the University had been effectively carried out by the department of Adult, Continuing Education and Extension with the available funds received for the purpose.

Problems Faced

In view of Extension the following problems have been faced:

- 'Extension' component—third dimension of higher education system has not been viewed seriously and not implemented effectively and adequately though it has been insisted by UGC, by all University Departments and colleges like Department of Adult, Continuing Education and Extension.
- Due weightage and recognition as prescribed by UGC has not been given to the 'Extension' activities carried out by the Faculty members and students attending interviews for appointment, promotion and award of honours.

- The existing Core Staff (Faculty) in spite of UGC guidelines, finds difficulties in getting redesignation as Reader and Lecturer.
- Non-availability of vehicle for transportation and non-availability of travelling allowance to the faculty members of Department of Adult and Continuing Education and Extension to undertake extension activities such as survey, training monitoring and supervision, evaluation etc. at grassroot level and to the places where 'Extension' programmes are implemented.
- Non-receipt of sufficient fund at the right time for implementing Extension programmes and its follow up programmes.

Future Directions for the Effective Extension of Extension Activity

The author of this chapter as a Faculty has been serving in the Centre for Adult, Continuing Education and Extension being involved in planning, programming budgeting, monitoring and supervision and evaluation of particularly Extension programmes for about two decades. Under these circumstances the following future directions are made for the effective and successful execution of the programmes under the third dimension 'Extension'.

- Suitable steps should be taken towards the conduct of Extension programmes not only by all the departments in the University but also the departments in the colleges.
- Due recognition and weightage (credits) should be given and it should be made mandatory to the extension activities carried out by the Faculty members and students attending interview for promotion, appointment and award of honour.
- Suitable steps to be made to provide vehicles for transportation to the faculties involved in implementing the Extension programmes.

- Sufficient funds should be provided at the right time for the Extension programmes and its follow up programmes.
- Orientation, refresher courses should be conducted periodically for the faculty members involved in implementing Extension programmes.
- Colleges also should be encouraged not only to implement Extension programmes but also to offer courses in Extension programme through Adult, Continuing Education and Extension Departments.
- Job opportunities for the qualified persons in Adult, Continuing Education and Extension should be created at college level.
- Post as 'Extension Officer' to be created at Government offices especially in agriculture, rural development, panchayat administration and social welfare and health departments for the persons qualified in Adult, Continuing Education and Extension disciplines.
- Honours and awards may be given for the Faculty members of Adult, Continuing Education and Extension who undertake the three dimension activities without vacation facilities throughout the year.

Conclusion

The impact of globalisation has placed a new demands on the education system and consequently transformation with rapid change is taking place in Asian regions particularly in India. Therefore 'Extension' should be made a compulsory component at all departments in Universities and colleges so as to prepare our students and youths to adopt change and learn new skills in accordance with the new demands of the world of work.

REFERENCES

1. Ray, G.L., (1996) *'Extension Communication and Management'* Naya Prakash, 206, Bidhan Sarani, Calcutta—700 006.

2. Supe, S.V. (1987) *An Introduction to 'Extension Education'*, Oxford and IBH Publishing Co. Pvt. Ltd. New Delhi.

3. University Grants Commission (1988), *A New Guide Lines on Adult and Continuing Education and Extension Programmes in University and Colleges*, UGC, New Delhi.

4. University Grants Commission (2004) *Tenth Plan UGC Scheme on Adult, Continuing Education, Extension and Field Outreach, Guidelines*, UGC, New Delhi.

5

Extension through Universities

A Perspective

B.S. Vasudeva Rao
P. Viswanadha Gupta

This is the Age of Extension. In all developing countries the fruits of knowledge, research and new skills have yet to reach millions of people who need it, who will be profited by it and whose contribution to the productive apparatus is immense. In this age highly advanced technology, we are talking of appropriate technology for the rural and tribal areas, so that they are not deprived of the wherewithal of their existence by the mighty currents of sophisticated production techniques. Appropriate technology is a means to promote individual and community self-reliance through a swadeshi movement. Not only in this country but in all other developing countries it is the cities and the urban areas which have gained importance and derived the advantages of the four decades of development initiated by the United Nations and other International agencies. Now we have changed our outlook and we are seriously thinking of Rural Development which will arrest the culture of too much urbanization and its attendant evils. In the world the present perspective of all governments are concerned with the well-being of the common man.

Dr. Malcolm, S. Adiseshaiah in his presidential address to IAPL conference pointed out "when we talk about rural development we are talking about National Development, as in rural development 80 per cent of the people supplying 70 per cent of the country's workforce and contributing 60 per cent of the National Product income are involved. To attain the goal of rural development abolition of unemployment within ten years, the needed is (i) wider ownership of rural assets, and (ii) a learning system which can help each rural unit to identify those resources in which it has comparative advantage and no village exists which does not have some such resources. This is the kind of innovative learning system which the goals of rural development system which can extend the benefits of knowledge and modern skills to the nook and corner of rural areas in various parts of the country."

As the UGC (1977) pamphlet on a policy frame on "Development of Higher Education in India points out of the university system has to discharge adequately its responsibilities to the entire educational system and to the society as a whole, it must assume extension as the third important responsibility and give it the same status as research and teaching." All Universities and colleges should develop close relationship of mutual services and support with their local communities.

The University Grants Commission (UGC), New Delhi framed the guidelines to extend the work on priority basis to following aspects:

- Human rights and rights of vulnerable groups
- Life Long and Continuing Education Programme at Grassroot level
- Community harmony and peace education
- Women empowerment through continuing education programme
- Social, environment and gender issues
- Panchayats and strengthens of local governance
- Health education for the community

University can be considered as a resource base with a wide variety of departments functioning as teaching units and also as knowledge generating units through research at various levels. When University has a large number of Departments in Humanities, Social Sciences, Natural Sciences, Physical Sciences, earth sciences, technology and Engineering, its obligation for extension is much more extension can operate at various levels. (1) Extension to other educational institutions at the lower level like colleges, high schools and primary schools, (2) Extension to other public institutions like industries, (small, medium and big) business houses, trade and commercial undertakings, transport and banking institutions and Government institutions (like Panchayats, Municipalities, urban development authorities) and training institutes (3) Extension to rural areas to increase their knowledge improve skill, increase productivity on different fronts, change their attitudes and thus finally bringing a new philosophy and Development, (change for better) and social action.

The above strategy gives the scope and extent of extension activity that can be carried by the University system and colleges. The University system with its brain power should look deeper into the problems of society and each university system should initiate a philosophy of reconstruction, development growth, change and lead the rest of humanity including the government, the local gentry the business and industrial organisations including Municipalities, Zilla Parishads, Panchayats and the development departments and welfare departments working at various levels. Unless and until the University system comes drawn from its ivory tower and jumps into a philosophy of action, there is no redemption for the enormous funds which we spend on various items of teaching, research and administration. They are not delivering the necessary goods at the present movement in the history of our nation.

The problems of the present day society are directly traceable to the lack of social philosophy of development sharing and utilising of the existing resources to the largest extent cooperation at various levels, co-ordination, reduction in the inequalities of income, productive and worthwhile programmes for generation of wealth, distribution of wealth, increasing the incomes of the lowest categories and thus reducing the poverty levels of the poorest of the poor and wholesale reconstruction of societal based on equality, fraternity, patriotism, national pride coupled with international outlook.

Need for Extension

The typical Indian community is lacking not only in materials resources, but also in human resources as well. When it comes to the question of community leadership, there is a vacuum which is actually a condition brought about by adult illiteracy and the inaccessibility of education to any but a small minority of youth. And those who studied successfully at higher level do not remain in their own communities for various obvious reasons. Therefore higher education has only a marginal impact on the local needs of manpower. The process of search for leadership in the community naturally leads to a closer examination of the human resources available there. Hence the alternative model of higher education called the extension education or community education or community college (Ramakrishnan: 1980) may well service the purposes pointed our earlier.

The primary focus of concern for the "extension education" is the community and its problems. Since a formal educational system cannot cater to the varied local needs, extension education can serve the varied complementary needs of the local community along with education. It must be a catalyst for self improvement and a locus for the varied community needs. The community school or extension education depends for its success not upon theories or upon building but upon people. Theories help, but the basic humanitarian concept upon which the community school depends for its success is more than a theory.

Taking education thus to the community is the goal of extension education. This new kind of education serving the entire community by breaking the access barriers has made life long learning a reality. But serving the entire community through community college is of course not an easy task. A difficult task like this can be a accomplished only by greater mobilization, organisation and planning at the community level for its development and service involving the community in which it is located or initiated. Recognition by the agency of extension education of its place in the community will have its effect on the curriculum, where social relevance is desirable, and on the responsibility and participation not only of parents and pupils but also of wider public. In return for the services and facilities which the agency of extension education is able to offer to the community, the agency will benefit by sharing the community facilities. This in turn may lead to further integration with other fields of education and youth work. In generating desirable changes in human behaviour in a given community, extension education adopts both informal and non-formal methods.

Need of Community College

The establishment of community colleges in urban, rural and tribal areas one way speeds up the objectives of extension education. The courses offered in the community college have to be in multi-dimensional nature to cater to the immediate needs of the local communities. The students who studied in the community colleges should be trained as agents of social change, get self employed or employed in the community and become useful and worthy citizens of society. The curriculum should include a large extent of liberal studies so that they can develop an analytical mind and begin to observe and understand the social process in and around the society. They should be able to create a new social order of peace, contentment, co-operation and dedication to work and share their knowledge and skills with other members of the society. They should be able to motivate the community in its scientific, literacy, cultural and artistic activities. The daily activity of the students, curriculum, instruction and teaching-learning process should be monitor and framed towards community service. Then only the objective will be realised.

If we trace the present malaise in our society and look to the international scene, we find that we have to attend to the following tasks immediately both in terms of a short and long range viewpoints initiating strategies of action on a war footing:

1. *Creation of Ecological Balance:* Already we see that some areas of the country are not receiving enough rainfall which can be traced to man's indiscriminate thinking with population pressure and urbanisation.
2. *Creation of New Energy System and Reviving the Old Energy Systems in Our Villages:* We suffer frequently due to inadequate supply of Electric power, diesel oil, kerosene, gas, firewood and charcoal. We have to plan at once to the need of boosting social forestry and economic forestry in all the banjar lands, village boundaries, converting hillocks into green pastures and raising of quick growing plants.
3. *Making best of existing water resources and discovery of groundwater resources*. We should not and cannot waste our water. Every drop of water should be utilized properly. Hence water management, crop rotation, multiple cropping, use of underground water resources, research in the use of aid and saline lands for cultivation becomes important.
4. *The White Revolution:* The green revolution has come. In consonance with development and use of land resources, the existing cattle wealth should be improved and the new varieties of Zersy, Murrah Swiss brown cattle development program should be encouraged.
5. *Subsidiary occupations and village industries*. All encouragement should be given for development of Poultry, Piggery, sheep units, silk industry, village crafts, handicrafts, palm jiggery, fruit preservation and canning and handicraft products.
6. We would develop intermediate technology where training youth with adequate skills with the help of financial institutions can start units for manufacture of soap, hair oils, tooth paste, leather goods, lime kilms cement, bricks, textiles and handlooms which should be taken away from big industry.

7. Abolition of illiteracy, ill-health and creation of scientific temper in society.
8. Creation of a new social ethic for building youth power and a philosophy of development should be promoted.

There are many more things that a university set-up of college can take up for Extension work through proper planning with schedules for 1 year, 2 years, 5 years and 10 years and gradually extend the extent of service it can render. It can extend the area of operations and the number of departments (staff and students) that can be actively involved in the Service of Society. Here the research scholars from the various departments of science, social science, Engineering and Technology can play the vital role. We will mention a few areas which University departments can take up as a long range plan for the next 5 years or for the next decade. The departments of Botany, Zoology, Ecology, Environmental science can jointly take up a scheme of educating villagers in social and economic forestry, water management, crop rotation, plant protection, agro industries, fisheries development and Ecological balance. They can select a group of 5 or 6 villages and concentrate their attention in bringing change by involving local youth, women and village elders.

The departments of physiology, Bio-chemistry, Pharmacy can take up extension in the field of foods, balanced diet, food preservation, healthy life, environmental sanitation and so on. The departments of Geology, Meteorology, Geo-physics, Geo-Engineering can take up schemes for exploration of minerals, groundwater, soil analysis, soil mechanics, setting of brick kilns etc. The departments of Physics, Chemistry, Engineering and Technology can take up development and use of alternative sources of energy, exploring new sources of energy and familiarity and use of Bio-gas, solar energy wind, energy, use of waste materials, preparation of sanitary pits, and compost pits, use of chemical fertilizers and natural manures. The departments for Economics, Applied Economics, Sociology, Social Work, Anthropology, Education and Psychology can appoint teams to make a study of socio-economic conditions, social and psychological problems, they can hold discussions and arrive at alternative strategies for social action, community service, community work and community planning. The villagers and slum dwellers can be provided courses of Non-formal Education. Formal Education, Adult Education to improve their knowledge, skills, change their attitudes and behaviour patterns for their social good, economic development and betterment. There should be continuity in education and social action.

The University administration can also extend its activities by training persons in office procedures, office management, typing, short hand, administration of small undertakings and other worthwhile and useful activities. The University as a whole should move, so that the Philosophy of extension permeates into all the departments and both the staff students and research scholars can plan and workout different strategies and undertake action programmes at suitable intervals of time. The motto "Where there is a will there is a way", can be implemented by suitably altering the time of admission, the vacations and the examination schedules, so that suitable programmes can plan throughout the year and also during vacations. The Indian Association for Adult Education, the Indian University Association for Continuing Education, the U.G.C and the State Departments of higher education by having a regional conference and identify one nodal university in each state for exploring the extension activities for a period of 5 years. The U.G.C. may earmark some fund to every department of the University to spent at last 10 per cent of its budget for extension work. Every state department of Higher Education in addition to nodal university and one or two colleges in the backward region to undertake extension activities, and share their experiences with others. The report should contain the approach they adopt towards extension, what action programmes were implemented, what were the difficulties faced, what was the outcome, so that the universities and the colleges can get feedback regularly and try to improve their extension services each year and also step up the pace of extension and gain more experience. Thus extension can gain ground slowly and steadily in the portals of the university and make headway in the coming decades.

REFERENCES

1. Adavi Reddy, A (1971) "*Extension, Education*" Srilakshmi Press, Bapatla.
2. Myrdal, Gunnar (1968) "*Asian Drama: A Inquiry into the Poverty of Nations*" 20th Century Fund, New York.
3. Ramakrishnan, G. (1980) "*A Community College for India*," The Institute for Development Education, Madras.
4. Subba Rao, D and Vasudeva Rao B.S (1984) "*Adult and Continuing Education: Some Perspectives*" Rural Development Publications, A.P.

6

Lifelong Education

Another Dimension of the University

G.V.R.R. Prasad

Wherever we go, we see the power of education to improve the lifestyles of people. For that matter no country was successful and developed without educating its people, that is how education is a key factor to sustaining growth and reducing poverty. We have good evidences of South Korea, Malaysia, Mexico and others in this direction which demonstrate that broadbased education is associated with a wide range of indicators of well being, including a nation's increased productivity and competitiveness as well as social and political progress. Most important is that, education is a basic human right that frees the spirit from the chains of ignorance and poverty. But unfortunately many people are still do not have access to proper education which will promises their livelihood, because of poverty, poor policies and corruption. Higher education apart from school education is undergoing radical changes and this has major implications for every aspect of university life. The universities in the country are in different stages of institutional renewal in order to match themselves with the new policies and other national and international imperatives, which include reorganising knowledge in disciplines into integrated programmes, increasing participation of students from a broader distribution of social groups and classes; and bring more responsive the social needs. The university should feel the impact of the challenges in the higher education environment comparing with the fulfillment of the requirements of the society very intensely. It should also set in motion a range of change processes to try to reposition the institution. One of such major ones should be livelihood-oriented lifelong learning.

Even among academics the concept of "lifelong learning" is certainly not a well understood term. There are very different views and ideological commitments on lifelong learning. In this regard lifelong learning presents an open ended alternative to the grand narratives in which "learning" is written over concepts like "struggle and development". We can understand that there is no closure neither formal nor informal to learning's and we have to base all our narratives on the proposition that there is no closure to learning. Higher education can function within the framework of lifelong learning to improve the democratic citizenship. Lifelong learning can help to sharpen the minds around the perennial questions as to the primary purposes of universities. We can argue and advocate that all our universities can be "universities of lifelong learning" ensuring quality. There is every need to encourage the people who work within university to be lifelong learners within a learning organisation. Lifelong learning is conceptualised in such a manner that research and scholarship is fore-grounded as the basis for the way in which an university engages with and helps to constitute the discourse of lifelong learning. We can think of an academic work as the scholarship of integration, (in writing text books) discovery, application and teaching, as such scholarship is very crucial in lifelong learning.

The idea of a "learning organisation" is a new one for most of the universities. According to Mr. Peter Senge, the key elements are systems thinking personal mastery, shared vision and team building. Learning organisations seek to improve performance through ongoing cooperative learning. Universities often affirm individualism rather than team-work on cooperation, and issues of organisational design and processes are usually not in focus. Organic processes rather dominated by bureaucratic agendas. As such lifelong learning is really challenging some fundamental paradigms about organisations.

Resource-based learning which is learner-centred has major implications for the curricula. The packaging of materials has major implications for delivery and for conceptions of what is being taught at present. Lifelong education (learning) encouraging more flexible approach, which also recognises prior learning, and emphasises access in terms of epistemology, time and space. Certainly a revolution will emerge in higher education which requires academies and administrators to be open to change. But most of the universities are just conservative. There is an argument that if the universities do not change they will become increasingly irrelevant as other institutions takeover their job. Tax payers may refuse to fund them. Therefore this is very important and vital for the universities to change their ways or serving the communities in the wider society. We need to understand this within the broader philosophical framework of lifelong learning. It is crucial that lifelong learning is not owned by or identified with any structure but it should be seen as a university vision itself. Lifelong learning encourages the traversing of traditional, professional domains like academic development, adult education, continuing education and higher education studies, which leads to new insights into faculty, students, curricula and organisational developments at the university and questions again the social purposes of the university locally and globally and the ways in which the institution relates to different communities.

This is a fact that we have to agree that the present system of higher education in India failed to cater to the educational needs of the community at grassroot level. Due to this fact only 7 per cent of the students who have completed their school education are enrolling for higher education according to official statistics. There is every need to increase this figure at least to 20 per cent, because in the present circumstances this is very difficult and almost not possible to get proper livelihood with school education qualification alone. In India the dropout rate of students in the age group of 11 to 17 years is more than 50 per cent. One of the main reasons for this dropout rate is that they do not see any guarantee that they will get a definite livelihood soon after the completion of their education. This is a peculiar situation we are facing that on one side we see due to globalisation lot of job opportunities in so many new fields are coming in front of us, on the other side there are about 40 million unemployed youth enrolled themselves in the employment exchanges. The reason for this pathetic and unfortunate situation in the country is due to defective education system of today. The youth of today are just wasting their time and energy by waiting themselves for white collar jobs and getting frustration if they fail in their endeavour. That is why we require a system of education which can provide work oriented/ experienced at secondary education stage itself.

Here the intension is not to criticise the present day education system of our country. No doubt our education system is good and producing great professors and scientists, doctors and engineers etc. but failed to produce ordinary skilled workers in various fields that are required to the community at grassroot levels. The skilled workers (vocational and technical) can start small scale industries at village and mandal level which can generate employment, and the community can become self-sufficient. This can be made possible by starting community colleges. The community college aimed at helping the rural, urban, tribal poor, woman and often disadvantaged to find gainful employment in collaboration with the local industry and community. Thus community college is the need of the day, and responds to the challenges of the excluded and eliminated from the formal system of education, and also provides an answer to the mismatch between education and employment capability, poverty, problems of unemployment and underemployment and dropouts of secondary and higher education level. The community college system can produce responsible citizens and promote job-oriented, work-related, skill-based and life-coping education. The key issue of community college system are equal opportunity, access, cost-effectiveness, flexibility in curriculum and teaching methodology. The community college should be so designed and arranged to cater to the needs of the student and community. The student may stop his education at any level and rejoin at any time and stage subject to is eligibility and ability. The courses offered in the community college should be capable of producing skilled and technical workers required and needed by the local industry, local vacations and suitable to the needs and situations of the local community and local service sectors.

There should not be any age restriction, and provide access to all age groups. If necessary the local artisans can also improve their vocational skills through the community colleges. The minimum age of admission into community colleges may be fixed at 15+ years, and no maximum age limit. The minimum qualification may be SSC pass or fail. The community college should have an established and approved structure/board which contains one principal, representatives or members nominated by State Govt. members from local bodies, members from local industry, members from higher education institution, members from National and State level research institutions. The most important is that every community college should necessarily have internship and job placement system within the local area, promotion of self employment and small business development, declaration of competence and eligibility for employment. The community college (system) can be considered as an alternative system of education which is different from the present day education system and providing technical education, skill up-gradation, employment to the rural poor. These community colleges should not placed/established at district or divisional or mandal headquarters, they should be in the villages only and accessible to the youth and community at village level. Some of the sources in community colleges are suggested hereunder:

1. Bore well/Pump/Motor mechanism
2. Two wheeler mechanism (Diploma, associate degree)
3. Four wheeler mechanism (Diploma, associate degree)
4. Pre-school teachers—Diploma, associate degree)
5. Fashion design (Diploma, associate degree)
6. Pottery (Diploma)
7. Office management, Secretarial Practice (Diploma, associate degree)

8. Web designing (Diploma)
9. D.T.P. (Certificate Diploma)
10. Air conditioning and Refrigeration (Diploma, associate degree)
11. Ticketing and travel management (Diploma associate degree)
12. Hotel management (Diploma, associate degree)
13. Bakery and Confectionery (Diploma, associate degree)
14. Footwear and leather goods manufacturing (Diploma, associate degree)
15. Beautician and healthcare (Diploma, associate degree)
16. Floriculture and horticulture (Diploma, associate degree)
17. Export/import trade management (Diploma, associate degree)
18. Organic farming (Diploma, associate degree)
19. Photography (Diploma)
20. Computer software (Diploma)
21. Computer hardware and maintenance (Diploma, associate degree)
22. Computer financial accounting (Diploma, associate degree)
23. Sales and marketing management (Diploma, associate degree)
24. Printing technology (Diploma, associate degree)
25. Electronics (Diploma, associate degree)
26. Small house appliances—Service and repair (Diploma)
27. Multipurpose rural development work (Diploma)
28. Medical laboratory technology (Diploma)

29. Medical radiography (Diploma)
30. Agro farming (Diploma, associate degree)

According to Mr. Xavier Alphonse, S.J. Who is director MCRDCE, the community college movement was started in the year 1995 with the Pondichery university community college. The first non-governmental organisation to start the Madras University college in 1996. Today we have 153 community colleges in 17 states, and helped 35,000 students from the socially, economically and educationally backward groups. Thus it has become a national phenomenon. The Madras Centre for Research and Development of Community Education (MCRDCE) Chennai, is the agency for promoting and implementing the concept in India. The MCRDCE has helped in the establishment and monitoring of 135 community colleges. It has conducted 15 teacher training programmes involving 1000 teachers from community colleges in India, and also conducted more than 100 workshops all over the country and four national consultations to propagate the concept. It has been also helping to establish community colleges abroad. The improved system has been accepted internally by the Association of American Community Colleges (AACC) and Community Colleges for International Development (CCID). However most of the community colleges have to be recognised by the state and central Govts. to facilitate horizontal and vertical mobility of their students. The National Institute of Open Schooling (NIOS) has given accreditation so far to 18 community colleges in the country. The national committee set-up by MHRD is preparing its recommendations to be submitted to Union Minister, and this system has found a mention in the Tenth Five Year Plan chapter 2.4 vocational education page 51. "There should be focus on convergence of schemes like the Sarva Sikha Abhiyan, the Adult Education, Vocational Education Programme at schools, ITIs, Polytechnic Community colleges etc.

If the Govt. comes forward to give recognition and accreditations to the community colleges, definitely the takers of higher education will increase preferably more from the socio-economically weaker sections. The universities as the research and guiding institutions of higher education may take lead to start more and more community colleges in the villages of their jurisdiction. If they take this step and initiation, this will be definitely a great service to the community.

REFERENCES

1. *Adult Education Development*, published by Institute of International Cooperation of the General Adult Education Association.

2. "Education for a Livelihood" By Mr. Xavier Alphonge S.J. Published in *Hindu* Paper on 20-12-2005.

3. "Bharatha Desamlo Samajika Vidya Vidhanam" by Mr. Ravi Kandadai, an article published in *Vidya-Vudyoga Vijayalu*—Telugu Fortnight Magazine November, 30, 2005.

7

Role of Universities in Promoting Sustainable Development Through Non-formal and Extension Education

Agenda for the 21st Century

S.C. Jhansi
Santosh Kumar Mishra

1. Introduction

As the globe has already entered into the 21st century, the Departments/Centres of Adult and Continuing Education and Extension (D/C of ACEE) in the Indian universities will have to focus more on strengthening the institutionalization of non-formal education through appropriate means. Thus, the D/C of ACEE need to highlight this particular aspect in the extension education (which has been recognised as *"third dimension of education"*) policy matters. In the context of 21st century situation, the concept of 'sustainable development' is of paramount importance. The D/C of ACEE of the Indian universities can play significant role in promoting sustainable development through non-formal/extension education channels.

"The collective power of people to shape the future is greater now than ever before, and the need to exercise it is more compelling. Mobilising that power to make life in the twenty first century more democratic, more secure, and more sustainable is the foremost challenge of this generation."

This chapter discusses the modalities for the purpose of prompting sustainable development through non-formal and extension education within the university system. In doing this, the paper addresses priorities for action at the systems level so that non-formal education becomes embedded within a wider and more diverse systemic framework.

"The entertainment media can play a role in raising the awareness of young children about a concept like sustainability. Such an effort must engage a wide range of stakeholders and yield benefits for all—most importantly, children."

"Systematic approaches are needed to help educational consumers, sort through and tie together the information resulting from everyday experiences. Strategies for the 21st century should attempt to articulate opportunities to craft non-formal educational experiences that enhance the ability of citizens to be better consumers, producers, policymakers, and stewards of the environment for their communities."

2. Thrust Areas for the Universities

- *Foster increased public awareness of sustainability through a public awareness programme:* A concerted public awareness effort will assist in gaining a firm grasp of the concept of sustainability and the practices that promote it. The programme should employ specific examples of everyday actions that are sustainable, descriptive, potential cumulative benefits associate with sustainable behaviour. If these efforts are successful, individuals will understand that these changes are worthwhile and have the potential to raise the quality of their lives. Easily understood information should be shared on a regular basis. This information should include relevant measures to gauge societal progress towards sustainability.
- *Support a system of regularly updated, comprehensible national benchmarks of progress toward the goals of sustainability:* Decisions that affects the long-term health and viability of communities are of utmost importance. These decisions are responses to growth and development

issues and the use and protection of natural resources. Individual citizens often sense a gap between their own day-to-day choices and the impact on events at the broader community, national, or global scales. With help from the media, a focused partnership aimed at informing the public about indicators of sustainability can help bridge this gap. The indicators can provide citizens with information that demonstrates individual contributions to the overall picture. Such efforts are under discussion, but no one best formula has been found to date. With further discussion, however, a system of benchmarks will emerge that can play a significant role in informing individuals.

- *Establish incentive programmes, such as national awards, to recognise successful partnerships within the business community that support educational efforts on sustainability:* The private sector, especially the business community, has been responsible for some of the most innovative programmes in the environmental and sustainable development arena. Nevertheless, university personnel struggle to establish successful partnerships to tap the expertise of the business and industry community. At the same time, businesses are searching to identify the best educational approaches. Incentives are needed to encourage and sustain partnerships and successes that are working. Recognition for those who are investing resources and creative energy in the formation and implementation of educational programmes can encourage others if they believe that their work will be publicly acknowledged.
- *Establish a national Sustainable Development Extension Network (SUDENET) to foster access to information, technical expertise, and collaborative strategies that result in action taken by local communities:* A new mechanism is needed that include but is not exclusively controlled by any one

existing extension entity. A redefined Sustainable Development Extension Network could employ services offered by diverse educational units such as community colleges, public schools, and private sector educational entities, as well as non-governmental organisations focusing on similar issues and priorities. At the same time, the new network can build upon the current infrastructure that exists in the country. The existing extension system could contribute to the new Sustainable Development Extension Network by providing technical assistance that brings together researchers who are:

(a) developing new technologies and those who adopt those new technologies;

(b) promoting sustainable development practices by providing information on sustainable alternatives and benefits;

(c) facilitating community visioning and planning processes; and

(d) providing access to current data and information available through electronics gateways.

A national Sustainable Development Extension Network could help provide bridges among areas of expertise in government agencies, universities, and colleges. To address the concerns of consumers, producers, communities, and individuals, a new collaborative strategy could be deployed among organisations that would provide assistance. A Sustainable Development Extension Network also would help ensure that local needs drive national policy; national policy and programmes are coordinated; and research, education, and extension roles for government and private sector agencies are clarified. Success ultimately will be assessed by the actions taken by local communities.

Visioning processes enable communities to plan for the long-term health of their communities and make decisions that will determine the economic viability of their communities. Many communities across the nation have taken this challenge seriously and are engaged in a process of visioning and assessment leading to strategic planning. Local decision-making can be enhanced with information and technical assistance from state and federal governments.

3. Management of Sustainable Development Extension Network

A Sustainable Development Extension Network should be coordinated with other initiatives. More specifically, the network could:

1. Assist in the implementation of a national effort to increase awareness of sustainability at the state and community levels.
2. Identify, document, and electronically link community civic groups, schools, business, and other entities interested in sustainable development.
3. Provide for local and state participation in the development of essential learnings in sustainability, design of community visioning and assessment process, student performance outcomes, criteria for curriculum development, and other standards.
4. Coordinate the efforts of major groups that design community visioning and assessment processes by documenting strategies and compiling results of such efforts.
5. Identify model programmes that satisfy agreed-upon standards of sustainable development.
6. Design and deliver training to organisations and individuals interested in applying principles of sustainability to their businesses, governments, projects, families, or schools.
7. Develop a five-year plan of action that targets specific geographic areas through a priority-setting process, and recommend public policy that enables the actions.

8. Develop a multidimensional matrix that includes environmental, economic and social components so each agency role will be maximised in terms of education, technical support, and financial assistance to specific geographic areas.
9. Coordinate the above functions with new and existing clearinghouses related to education for sustainability across the country.

The proposed action plans, management structure, funding mechanism, and evaluation indicators for the Sustainable Development Extension Network are based on shared decision-making and leadership, coordinated actions, individual and collective organisational accountability for funds and programme outcomes, and management for results. Although the goal might be reached more quickly through unilateral investment in a single organisational entity, the national goal of sustainable development requires a more comprehensive strategy.

"Non-formal education offers hands-on experiences as well as more traditional modes of learning. As indicated by the Commission on Global Governance, the need for these non-formal educational experiences is urgent."

4. Implementation Strategies

Representatives from the participating agencies as well as state consortia should direct a process to determine how a Sustainable Development Extension Network can best be managed, staffed, and financed. The process should be coordinated with the national policy recommendations. This process should result in:

(a) the development of accountability indicators;
(b) collection of data;
(c) analysis of results; and
(d) formulation of recommendations and conclusions concerning a Sustainable Development Extension Network.

The formation, structure, management, leadership, and implementation of a Sustainable Development Extension Network could be based on the following principles:

- Research-based technology is generated and applied as determined by community needs.
- Transfer of technology to communities and individuals is based on an appropriate combination of education plus technical and financial support aimed at user adoption.
- Management processes for identifying needs, setting priorities, and building collision and partnerships are inclusionary.
- Targeted and focused assistance responds directly to local communities and needs.
- Existing research, education, and extension management and delivery systems are utilised, redefined, and expanded.
- Alternative implementation strategies and organisational participation models are provided.
- Consistency in substance among programmes and the results from programmes are based on a verified set of principles and outcomes.
- Management and design of the structure and process are not dominated by any one entity, but developed through a collaborative process of defining common goals and unique organisational roles.

Establish an extension network to enhance the capacity of individuals, workforces, and communities to live sustainability.

5. Policy Recommendation

- Expand public access to opportunities to learn about sustainability issues as they relate to the private, work, and community lives of individuals.
- Support a campaign to raise public awareness of sustainability, convey information on indicators of

sustainable development, and encourage individuals to adopt sustainable practice in their daily lives.

A successful extension network would empower individuals in communities to shape their own futures through an appropriate mix of:

- education;
- technical assistance; and
- *fiscal support.*

Extension networks give individuals the tools to control their own futures, while providing data and information, educational expertise, and needed financial assistance.

6. Summing up

In today's world, information about the global environment and sustainable development is increasingly available through television, print media, telecommunications networks, and commercial, software products. Using this information, the universities can make decisions about day-to-day actions on what to buy and what to do about issues that affect their communities. Although the public has a heightened awareness of sustainability issues and is responding by making wise decisions regarding those issues, the process of sifting through information is not as easy or helpful as many would like. Unclear messages increase the difficulty of encouraging an individual (or targeted audience) to engage in action or make informed choices.

"Young people around the world are playing a role in monitoring progress towards sustainable development through various efforts. Youth can help measure progress toward building and maintaining healthy communities. School groups, individuals, community groups, and families should be invited to participate in the sustainable development project."

Yardsticks for measuring nation's progress toward sustainability and staying in touch with the impacts of day-to-day actions on natural and built environments, economic growth and social systems are vital. Such efforts can benefit from media attention and support from groups working cooperatively to raise the collective awareness and knowledge base of the public. Only then can the public's understanding of the meaning and importance of sustainability be enhanced.

Encourage partnerships and activities that support community visioning and assessment activities.

The university system has to struggle to develop and implement the requisite curricula to teach youngsters about the importance of sustainability and its relationship to quality of life. Business, community groups, and professional organisations have engaged in this dialogue and have been quick to realise that more information is needed.

National support can include:

- facilitating the exchange of ideas by providing appropriate and timely information about successful models for replication;
- training of leaders for visioning processes; expansion of local, regional, national and international visioning networks; and
- engagement of communities across the nation in integrated, holistic approaches to long-term planning for sustainable communities.

If the public is to become more involved in local sustainability issues, support mechanism are needed to:

- translate research information;
- transfer new technologies, introduce educational strategies;
- develop public policy; and
- organise at the community level to chart sustainable courses of action.

A national programme could include the following four components:

— Identifying and compiling examples of visioning processes that have been successful in communities;

— Designing and developing a workbook and other resource materials for dissemination to interested communities to serve as a guidebook for action and planning at the community level;

— Establishing a Leadership Institute for Sustainable Communities to train leaders in facilitating cooperative planning by diverse stakeholders; and

Encourage lifelong learning about sustainability at the individual, household, and community levels.

8

Extension as Third Dimension for the Universities

Present Status, Problems and Future Directions

J.P. Dubey

University extension is under operation through the intervention of University Grants Commission by its Policy Frame on Higher Education (1977). In its 28 years of continuing effort to establish a link between university and community, the university extension has undergone several transformations including creating an interface between these two and generating some insight from the real life situation. And in doing so it has encountered several problems. This chapter attempts to deal with the key concepts and issues related to extension: third dimension, status, problems and future directions. The University Grants Commission has declared extension as the third dimension of university function. The three dimensions are teaching, research and extension. Three dimensions mean an object or a concept having or appearing to have length, breadth and depth, sufficiently full in characterisation of events to be believable. Teaching and research having established itself as the two dimensions of university function, extension is still in process of gaining the status of third dimension.

Extension as the 'third dimension' is an umbrella term which includes the organisation of adult education, continuing education, population education extramural lectures, legal literacy, science for the masses, community education and awareness through field outreach activities like short-term training and skill development courses by the institution of higher education. There are different terms in use which explains the extension activities. However terminological differences do not affect the general understanding and contents of the programme planning and delivery of services by the service providers to the beneficiaries. It is convenient to understand the concept of extension in its historical growth and the role it performs. Authors have attributed different meanings and use to the term. The activities and services provided by the university system have also been known by different names, in different countries and also at different times, such as extramural studies, continuing education, outreach, university adult education, community college, folk schools, etc. To explain all these activities in the university a generic term 'university extension' has emerged which incorporates various aspect of work intended and performed by the university other than the established job of teaching and research.

In India university extensions has grown with the literacy programme in the form of eradication of illiteracy programme. Universities also attempted to understand adult illiterates for their educational needs, their psychological process, learning potential, their learning reference point, and readiness in order to enrich the programme. This was in line with the Paulo Friere's comment on the adoption of total approach as "in approaching to educate adult illiterates, the educator must 'die' as exclusive educator of the educate in order to be 'born' again as educates of the educatee. Once an organised initiation of the activities and the institution of the departments of adult, continuing education and extension was in principle agreed the organisational structure, role, its relationship with other faculties were debated at various forum and a significant input was provided by Mehta (1965), Bengal Social Services League and Indian Adult Education Association (IAEA), and Indian University Association for Continuing Education (IUACE). To begin with the programme of eradication of illiteracy' was the best way to initiate this process in general higher education institutions. The votaries of university doing extension were of belief that productivity was the victim of current form of education at every level and adult extension education provides two things: it is education as generally understood plus a discovery on the part of individual that he is capable of much more than he believed himself to be. For others it was clearly stated in the UGC guidelines 1983 that the institutions of professional education where teaching-learning-examination system is not like general education should be asked to contribute in special ways.

With the historic pronouncement under the 'policy frame' of 1978, which envisaged the involvement of students and teachers in a planned manner for acceleration of interaction with the community by way of extension work, some 18000 centres by the end of 1985 in the first phase and over 50000 centres by the second phase in 1990 was established. The year 1986-87 saw to it that there were 25,824 adult education centres spread over 92 universities. By the end of 1988 there were 104 universities entrusted with the job of extension through DACEEs/CACEEs to extend knowledge generated in the universities and enabling the university faculty to interact with the community in order to enrich their own knowledge and effect changes in the university's teaching learning process. The UGC policy led to the massive expansion of university extension at a very rapid pace during 1980s when these agencies grew in terms of programme content and number of personnel's and a huge involvement of the universities and colleges in NAEP generated renewed interest in the nature of relationship between not only the university/college and its surrounding community but also between the agencies directly responsible for this programme as well as others in the university.

The programme of University Extension through DACEEs/CACEEs in the form of adult education, continuing education, population education and other forms is in its operation since 1978 barring a few like Rajasthan, Poona, Tirupati and Madras where these programmes were introduced a little earlier at different time in between 1965-1973 and teaching programme were launched in Poona (1965), Rajasthan (1967), Tirupati (1976) and Madras (1977). The major thrust to the programme was given after acceptance of literacy as an important input of development when National Adult Education Programme was made part of the Minimum Need Programme (MNP) and 93 universities took up the cause of adult extension education by introducing the units/centres of Adult and Continuing Education and Extension. To understand the functioning of these structures in university system some efforts were made through Review Committees of University Grants Commission (UGC) sponsored studies, and independent reviews.

The process of operationalisation of extension developed some models, specific programmes, and implementation strategies. In search of these the Indian University Association for Continuing Education (IUACE) organised a national workshop on "preparation of models, programmes and implementation strategies in adult and continuing education". Operationalisation models were also suggested (Bhatia and Dubey: 1989). Based on the reports of review committees in 1997 UGC categorised these extension structures in three phases for funding purposes as well as their performance in preceding plan period.

Status

These departments/units have been given a structure in the university system either in form of a centre, unit, department or a faculty depending on the level of their structural and functional compatibility in the university system and these are engaged in teaching research and extension with the help of functionaries directly associated with the departments or with the help of other functionaries associated with the programme based on their expertise and extension needs.

The extension departments consist of core faculty of Director, Assistant Director and Project officer. There has been some difficulty noticed in these agencies as far as their nomenclature and functions were concerned. The nomenclatures were not exactly in consonance with the existing system of the universities and adequate efforts were not made to convince the universities of their validity in the university system. The absence of recognition of such designations led these agencies to work in the direction of harmonising the nomenclature in tune with the existing system of the university in order to minimise the difficulties in the day-to-day functioning. Several universities initiated this move. Delhi, Tirupati and Madras were first to harmonise the designation of director with the professor in 1984 but the process of harmonising the designation of the functionaries like assistant director and project officer with reader and lecturer or any other was not done till 1997 in some universities while others are yet to do it. The point on which the advocacy of this re-designation hinged was the basic differences that existed in the universities which kept on hindering the growth of both activities as well as the personal.

The problems faced by the DACEEs / CACEEs can be better understood only after having an overall impression of contribution made by these units. The DACEEs / CACEEs have been able to make some contribution in the realm of higher education, which can be grouped in following heads:

- Finding a place in the system of higher education. From the stage of an experiment to the level where these agencies have started contributing to the overall university practices either in the form of *resource generation through the market based continuing education programmes or helping the university to meet the social responsibility by developing and conducting need based courses for the general community.*
- *Successfully experimenting with the idea of University-Community interaction and development of insights* into the real life situations of the common people. The respondent universities were found to be benefiting from the progressive higher mobilisation of students and teachers towards extension activities both to benefit themselves as well as benefit the community.

- *Developing the area of study of 'Extension'* which has till date been treated as an area of practice. The agencies and the other respondents were found to be actively engaged in the work of developing the discipline by undertaking researchers and projects in areas of literacy, population, capacity building and organised behaviour both independently as well as with the help of other faculties.
- *Since the potential of adult extension education lies in strengthening of learning components of individual as well as communities for democratic development or social transformation, the obstacle to it are in all probability the same which inhibit all other transformative social process.* Adult extension education has been a struggle. Various forms of adult extension education grew out of the changes taking place in socio-economic spheres and treated as a way of ameliorating the worst excesses (Budd Hall) of savages on one hand, opportunities for workers to learn aspects of dominant culture education and on the other as a support for social movement activists to learn how to work together to create social legislation in the fast developing countries and as a measure of intervention to reduce the social and economic tensions in the traditional ridden countries.
- It is noticed that there has been *upward movement in the growth and distribution of DACEEs between 1982-1990 and there is a perceptible fall in the number of universities providing extension services from 1992-1998.* There were 104 universities offering extension services in 1988 which fell down to 73 in 1998. The argument put forward by the stakeholders are varying with the university. It is found to be associated with the quality of functionaries, decline in state funding, leadership issues both at the university level as well as UGC level and uncertainty of personnel's job. *The analysis of the given situation*

> *points to the fact that these institutions were continuously under some sort of struggle and lacking a policy base both within and from outside and that is why these institutions either lost the continuity of thought and practice provided during the initial years or these were submerged in the struggle for resources and a continuing worry of their own marginality.* There is a need of creating an environment where extension becomes as much part of the social and educational policy either at the institution level or macro-national level then only it will survive and succeed.

These could be identified as problems related to the concept of extension, its acceptance by the university community, non-acceptance of the multiple designation system, accommodation of nontraditional roles and approaches, globalisation and creating a different set of evaluation system for the functionaries by respective universities. Since the programme was intended to benefit both the community as well as the university the process of understanding community in the context of programme should have preceded its formalization. In absence of it the programme has to borrow heavily from the other agencies involved in extension and depend on the vision of its leaders and the UGC Guidelines. Consequently the Guidelines and programmes became the subject of study for several researchers and no efforts were made to analyze the problems and strength of extension. The above staged problems need to be looked in the correct perspective. An attempt has been made in the remaining part of the paper to understand the problems especially in the context of concept of extension, possibility of accommodating multiple designation system and globalisation.

The conceptual limitation is the one of the major obstacles which hindered the growth of adult extension education. The conceptual limitation implies that there is a lack of agreement among the academicians in order to develop roles and approaches for extension functionaries. Some focused on study and practice, other saw to it in reference to power relation, Paulo

Friere saw to it as a liberation process in the form of popular education. Even Budd Hall agrees that lack of theoretical development has disabled the forward move of adult extension education. Theoretical contributions from political economy, critical theory, feminism, popular education etc. are the recent additions to the theoretical framework. The extension system has envisioned the developmental pattern from 'individual to universal' as opposed to the concept of 'universal to individual, professed by globalization.

Globalization has very few options for the extension and extension like activities as it has it in entrenched into the concept of dominance and low regard to experience and local culture. The only benefit it offers to the extension is advocacy of adopting and applying the tested programmes and methods by the functionaries and implements the same in their respective area of work. Bennet C.F. in his new Interdependence Model suggests that extension (in USA) has a comparative advantage in performing the role of education rather than the role of transfer. Extension is for liberation of people which cannot be by a consciousness and knowledge other than own (False Bonda, 1991). In a situation where society if categorized by the pattern of consumption (a globalisation phenomenon) the 'Rich man's basket' of six per cent in number and consumes forty per cent of the goods and services (Das Gupta, 1979: 5). This consciousness in itself is not sufficient to warrant liberation as the communication process and theory building by the same four per cent of which is termed as 'Grand collision' blames the victims and finds fault with them and work for social action designed to change not the society but rather victims.

To fulfill the extension priorities as enunciated in the policy frame of 1977 and also envisioned in the Tenth Plan guidelines in the face of changing pattern of funding and processes of globalization there could be two strategies. one is to accept the discourse that globalization is inevitable and irreversible and amend the approach and philosophy of adult extension education and allow it to be governed by the rule of law of competitiveness and economic forces and divorcing it from its time tested approach of being a programme of intervention for helping the marginalised and vulnerable groups and second is to appreciate it's implication on various development communication and adult extension education and resist its involvement of nations/states/people grappling with poverty, vulnerability and prevent further marginalization of such group.

Since the first strategy clearly suggests to follow the course of globalization and to effect changes in the programme of adult education in the light of recent technological innovations and surplus capital available to be invested in the programme of adult education. With the free flow of capital and network services the possibility of improving the condition and quality of adult extension education is certainly high. This may also help in creating a system of better training vis-à-vis changing world of work. This process can be accelerated because of the compression of time and space (a globalization affect). The second strategy envisions appreciation of the impact of globalization on adult education correctly and adopts ways to resist it and does not allow further marginalization of the vulnerable (passive nation/state/group/individual). Because with the increased flow of capital the private initiative are on the rise and progressive withdrawal of state funding to the programmes of even basic nature of providing basic literacy and basic health are in of being displaced by such education and health facilities which are meant for chosen few. The process of generating a critical thinking and reflexivity (an extension agenda) planning for self system of dialogue, would all be a victim of a centralised, all powerful globalization phenomenon.

Adult education may not find it easy to compete with the training needs and provision available in the fast changing development world. With meanings of economizing progressive withdrawal of state funding and private capital-inflow adult extension education may finds it's relevance sliding and power to experiment/innovative being replaced by implementation and replication of the content (already decided) and as modifier of the context (as suitable to the global concern) and a tool in the progress of homogenization.

Both the strategies of modifying the adult extension education in tune with the globalization or resisting the globalization to save adult education and extension, seeks for a proper analysis and development of suitable strategies to cope with the fast changing technology economy and knowledge. The institution's of higher education may find the clash of interest in other areas of pursuit of knowledge of a low magnitude but in the case of extension it is not so. With a certain degree of autonomy and huge intellectual resource higher education institute needs to regroup their efforts in either case so that the adult education as a field of study and practice does not meet a fate extinction and a new function of extension acquired by universities along with teaching and research, to meet its social responsibility does not relegated to background with the fast changes let loose by the globalization. The globalization offers both threat as well as opportunities. The threat of a sustained withdrawal of funding to such services which are not directly the mainstream jobs of the universities would adversely affect the training, skill development, individual interest promotion program intended to enrich the individual rather than harmonize the individual with the dominant socio-economic culture of the developed countries. All social, economic or political institutions evolve and exist in a system, and not a vacuum, so there can not be immune to change in the larger environment. Hence developing a response system, to both the processes of a dominant discourse as well as an objective reality is imperative upon the extension mechanism in higher education. The long cherished goals of extension as an intervention programme of education and services to help the marginalized and vulnerable in such a way that the concept of education for all: both in terms of equity and equality is achieved. The Universities has a major role to play in this process of either resisting or modifying the process in such a way that the fundamentals of adult extension education both as a field of study and field of practice is not rendered worthless in the era of fierce competition and economic control.

Future

This is also equally important to take note of the fact that the motive behind the establishment of extension centres in the higher education system was not only to create a department of an identified discipline engaged in teaching and research but to act as an interface between university and community. This is possible only when these units keep their roots, i.e. community intact with it and continue to act as a dynamic institution always ready to innovative and adopt newer ways of development. Future extension need assessment at all India level is needed because this extension unit found it difficult to innovate under the compulsion of meeting target. The strength of extension unit found it difficult to innovate under the compulsion of meeting target. The strength of extension lies in the fact that a continuous assessment of university expertise and knowledge need of the community is matched in form of innovative programme. The issues of contemporary nature like environmental concern in form of green literacy (Usang N. Eva, 1992) as the skill of transmitting and receiving information in an intelligible manner with sustainable environmental elements built in, societal concerns like social and distributive justice, legal literacy, training, requirements of disadvantaged group of students in form of preparatory coaching for services, teaching and instruction for deaf and dumb, women centred various entrepreneurially courses, rural development courses etc. must find concerns in the university system as a sustainable response towards the society.

Regular assessment of priorities and programmes need to be undertaken by the extension centres either independently or in unison in order to identify newer areas of human concern. Besides the youth's human resource development need, which is being fulfilled by the continuing education programmes of the university extension the older people are emerging as a major area of extension concern. There educational, emotional and social concerns could find a place in extension agenda. Developing continuing education programme for such group would meet both the extension concern of productive aging as well as meeting the financial uncertainties in extension. DACEEs/CACEEs in Indian Universities have taken lead in those areas where traditional faculties have not been forthcoming. These Departments/Centres have been able to make reasonably good progress in the attainment of some objectives by being successful in establishing and sustaining a system of intervention at the level of university which has never been accepted as a genuine form and function of the universities. The organised extension lectures lead to an institutional association in adult literacy programme which in turn invited the attention of both academicians/researchers and administrators and laying the foundation of emergence of an area of both practice as well as study in higher education. The concern and sensitivity shown by the universities through DACEEs/CAEEs reflect in the acceptance of short term/non-evaluative/non-credit courses in form of general to specific concerns speaks about the turn around in the thinking of the universities.

REFERENCES

1. Lauzon A.C. *Extension Education Reconsidered: Implication of the Idea of Sustainability* ISSN 0835-4626 No. 12, 1997.
2. Report of National Workshop on Preparation of Models, Programmes and Implementation Strategies in Adult and Continuing Education, November 13-15, 1981, Ahmedabad, IUACE.
3. Singh Amrik (1980), *Adult Education As Liberation in Some Critical Considerations in Adult Education,* University of Delhi, pp. 12-13.
4. J.P. Dubey (2005), University Extension and Globalization, *Journal of Higher Education,* Vol. 43, No. 33, published by Association of Indian Universities, New Delhi.
5. Bennet C.F., A New Interdependence Model: Implications for Extension Education: *Journal of Extension Systems*. 1994. 10:1, 33-45; 12.
6. Bhatia S.C. (1980) *Linking Extension with Curriculum, Some Critical Considerations in Adult Education*, p. 45. University of Delhi, New Delhi, 1980.
7. Ms Mehta, Key Note Address to First All India Conference and University Adult Educate, July 1965, Bhopal.
8. Adult Education Components in the Development Schemes of Govt, of India. A Compendium. Directorate of Adult Education 1986.
9. Kundu C.L., *Adult Education*, Sterling Publishers, New Delhi.
10. *University System and Extension as the Third Dimension*; Report of the Review Committees Appointed by UGC, New Delhi 1987, page 118.

11. Malcom, S. Adiseshiah, Adult Education Development and NAEP *Journal of Indian Adult Education Association*, October-November, 1979 and p. 15.

12. Satish Chandra (1984) The University Grants Commission and its Role: A Review, *Journal of Higher Education,* Vol. 10, No. 1.2 1984, New Delhi.

13. *Guideline for Department / Centre for Adult Continuing Education and Extension Work and Field Outreach*, University Grants Commission (Reprint 2002), New Delhi, pp. 5, 6.

14. Pillai K.S.: Research in Adult Education, Past Present and Future in *Journal of Indian Adult Education Association,* Vol. 54, No. 2: pp. 25-26, IAEA, New Delhi 1993.

15. *University System and Extension as the Third Dimension*, Report of the Review Committee appointed by the University Grants Commission, New Delhi (1986).

16. Kundu C.L. (1994): *Adult Education Programme in the University System*, Nirmal Book Agency, Kurukshetra University.

17. Latika (1995) The Development of Adult Continuing and Extension Education in Universities of Maharashtra State during Post-Independence era Ph.D Thesis, Department of Education, Punjab University, Chandigarh.

18. *UGC IX Plan Guidelines on Adult Continuing Education and Extension and Field Out Reach*, University Grants Commission, New Delhi, p. 28, Annexure iv, 1997.

19. Mukerjee. B (1961) *Community Development in India* p. 33, Orient and Longman, New Delhi.

20. Collins I. & Bolt R.K. 2003 (quotes) in *Literacy, Literacies, Text Power and Identity*, p. 15, Cambridge, New York.

21. Friere, Paulo (1968, 1970) *Pedagogy of the Oppressed*, New York, Salisbury.

22. Obibuka, L.U (1983), *Agricultural Extension as a Strategy for Agricultural Transformation*, Nasukka, University of Nigeria Press.

23. Friere Paulo (1973) *Extension or Communication*, The Salisbury Press, New York

9

Extension Education in Indian Universities

Overview

Bhalba Vibhute

Introduction

The UGC Policy Statement (1977) had underlined the need of the extension activities as a important dimension of higher education equal in importance with teaching and research and thenceforth the movement of establishing Departments of Adult and Continuing Education in Indian Universities geared up. As inseparable part of the community, universities have to serve the society and especially cater to the educational needs of society. The extension dimension adopts the approach of reaching to the masses. It is, in this regard, in recognition with the role of these department the UGC policy of 1977 says, "If the university system has to discharge adequately it's responsibilities to the entire education system and to the society as a whole it must assume extension as a third important responsibility and give it the same status as research and teaching." The Conference of Vice-Chancellor's (May 1981) ondorsed fully the concept of extension education as a third dimension of higher education in India.

Journey

Though the University Grants Commission's efforts of starting Adult and Continuing Education activities in Indian Universities, started in 1960, the momentum of establishing such departments geared up in eighties. The UGC policy Statement of 1977 and the Conference of Vice-Chancellors of 1981 and also the report of the expert group for the evaluation of poverty under the chairmanship of Dr. M.S. Swaminathan (1982) had enabled the UGC for formulating guidelines for undertakings the activities of extension education in Indian Universities.

1982

The UGC prepared guidelines of Adult and Continuing Education and Extension Work and circulated to all universities in India in 1982. The emphasis of the guideline was of starting continuing education activities by the Indian universities. By organising continuing education activities in the universities it was expected that the universities will be able to establish necessary linkages with the community for fostering the social change, providing opportunities for disseminating knowledge in all walks of life, catering to the felt needs of all sections of the society to secure their effective participation in development process, enriching higher education in integration with higher education programmes in the system, providing an opportunity to the faculty and the students to exposition of field experiences and faculty and students participation in action research. To fulfill these objectives 1982 guidelines had suggested some programmes. These programmes were categorised in four sections.

1. Awareness generating general interesting programmes.
2. Development of basic education and skills.
3. Imparting an empowering skills and professional know-how.
4. Developing co-curricular linkages.

1983

The Government of India launched National Adult Education Programme (NAEP) on 2 October, 1978 for making illiterate persons in the age group of 15-35 literate and providing to them skills for self-directed learning leading to self-relevant and to play active role in their own development and in the development of their environment. The NAEP policy of 1978 had explained it's approach of looking towards Adult Literacy Programme in the following words:

> "The problems of poverty and illiteracy are two aspects of the same stupendous problem and the struggle to overcome one without at the same time waging a fight against the other is certain to result in aberrations and disappointments. For this reason, NAEP is visualised as a means to bring about a fundamental change in the process of socio-economic development: from a situation in which the poor remain passive spectators at the fringe of the development activity to being enabled to be at its centre, and as active participants. The learning process involves emphasis on literacy, but not that only; it also stress the importance of functional up-gradation and of raising the level of awareness regarding their predicament among the poor and the illiterate."

To take review of the National Adult Education Programme a committee under the Chairmanship of Professor D.S. Kothari was appointed by the Govt. of India, (1980). That committee had to recommend modifications for improvement of Adult Education Programme for its better implementation. Kothari Commission had felt the need of larger participation of students in the Adult Education Programme and therefore, recommended that universities and colleges should be recognised as implementing agencies of NAEP. The role of universities and colleges in implementation of NAEP has been explained by the Commission as Universities and Colleges should be involved to the greatest possible extent, through NSS or otherwise. Involvement of women's colleges whould help in increasing the participation of women learners in the Programme. In the long run participation in social service, including adult education should become a part of the academic course.

As per the 1977 policy of the UGC, UGC had taken steps in organising activities in extension education and accordingly

1982 guidline was also circulated to the universities in India. The Govt. of India had initiated action in organising adult literacy programme throughout the country and made provisions of spreading of Universal the elementary education for the age group of 14-16, with special emphasis on girls and simultaneously involving students and voluntary agencies in the programme for the removal of adult illiteracy, in point no. 16 of New 20 Point programme. The UGC, in-consultation with the Govt. of India, appointed a Working Group under the Chairmanship of Dr. Mrs. Madhuri R. Shaha, Chairperson of UGC in 1982 to review the on going programmes of adult education and extension through universities and colleges and to suggest a dynamic programme on point No. 16 of the new 20 point programme of the Government of India. The Working Group under the leadership of Dr. Mrs. Madhuri R. Shaha, consisting of 16 members reviewed the on going programmes of the UGC and prepared guidelines for the implementation of Point No. 16. The working group laid emphasis on teachers, students involvement in adult literacy programme. The group felt that the objectives of the programmes should aim at plan involvement of universities and colleges in the eradication of illiteracy, of promoting the process of interaction of universities/ colleges with the community, providing special attention towards programme for under-privileged strata of the society, relating the programmes directly to the needs, interests, aspirations and life situations of the learners, helping learners in acquisition of basic literacy skills, conducting post-literacy and continuing education activities, providing infrastructural facilities and having effective monitoring and evaluations methodologies. The report of the Working Group entitled "Report of the UGC Working Group on Point No.16 of the New 20 Point programme of the Govt. of India" (1993) adopted centre-based literacy programme approach for eradication of illiteracy and suggested a model of involvement of universities and colleges in this programme. Report also suggested that department of Adult Education, the NSS and NCC units of the concerned universities should try to involve large number of teachers and students of the universities and the affiliated colleges in the programme of eradication of adult illiteracy. The report also highlighted different patterns, which include norms of assistance, staffing pattern, release of grants, continuation in assistance etc. In the major recommendations the working group had suggested that teaching, research and extension to be given equal importance. A single mechanism be created in the university system under umbrella approach, Staff of the DACEE is to be appointed immediately for smooth functioning of the programme, adult education should be included as a compulsory subject in teacher training courses, prompt media support be sought, and universities should utilize the experts in pedagogy/androgogy and behavioral science departments for the trainers. In short 1983 guideline suggested that for better results continuity, flexibility, co-operation, recognition, training, monitoring, evaluation post-literacy follow-up and research etc. should be given due importance.

1984

The policy-makers at the UGC level decided to enlarge the activities in extension education and hence in 1984 the scheme of Population Education Clubs (PEC) in the universities and colleges was prepared and the responsibility of organizing activities in this sphere was entrusted with the DACEE in Indian Universities. The objectives of this scheme were as follows:

1. to make the student community aware of the dynamics of population and to enable them to understand the determinants and consequences of the population problem;
2. to make the students understand the population policies and programmes of the country and appreciate the need for "Small Family Norm" ; and
3. to educate the community about the consequences of rapid population growth at the family and national levels.

In accordance with these objectives universities were advised to organize different type of activities.

To monitor the activities of population education of different states, the UGC, in 1987, established 12 Population Education Resource Centres (PERC) and added 5 more such centres in 1996 (total 17) as UGC-UNFPA project on population and development education in higher education system. The DACEEs in the country under the leadership of respective PERCs implemented programmes of population education up to 2002 but in 2002 PERCs became dys-functional due to stoppage of financial assistance from UNFPA.

1985

In continuation with to the programming of eradication of illiteracy continuing education and population education in the year 1985 UGC added one more component in the activities of the department namely Scheme of Planning Forum in universities and colleges. Following two fold objectives were identified for this purpose by the UGC:

(i) To create an awareness of need for planned development of the country among the student community and involve them in national development efforts right from the planning stage.

(ii) To develop plan consciousness among the educated youth in particular and through them among the general public.

It was expected that planning forum should work as repository of plan literature, serve as a plan information centre, identify local as well as regional needs to strengthen planning process, work as feedback agency regarding the implementation of the plan, organize awareness programmes and adopt villages for integral rural development, etc. Due to the policy decision taken by the DOC this activity was shifted from DACEE to the departments of Economics of Indian Universities in 1988.

1986

In the year 1986 Govt. of India declared its National Policy of Education and in its Programme of Action it emphasized the scheme of Mass Programme for Functional Literacy (MPFL). The main objective of this programme was involvement of students and teachers in universities and colleges in eradication of illiteracy and the approach adopted in this scheme was very flexible. In this scheme it was expected that one student should identify one or two or five illiterate adults and make them literate by inducting teaching, learning activity. Under the MPFL the literacy course was to be imparted for approximately 150 hours by the student volunteer.

1988

In accordance with the UGC policy, the UGC periodically conducts review of the activities under the third dimension and hence UGC appointed a committee to take review of the performance of DACEEs and later on the report of this committee was published in 1988 in the form of guidelines. This guideline identified the new approach, keeping in view National Policy on Education of 1986. The UGC decided that universities and colleges should adopt area-based approach "The area development approach envisages inter-linkages of the existing programme of removal of illiteracy, continuing education etc. with other activities as an extension programme in the community for achieving critical development goals and to set up demonstration units in area adopted by the universities/ colleges". The critical development goals particularly include eradication of illiteracy, continuing education programmes, population education for improving quality of life, legal literacy., science for the people and other welfare and integrated community developmental activities. The area development approach would thus require institutions to resort to a sharing and networking approach. The 1988 guideline had recommended that each university should develop an integrated approach and adopt area-based programmes which includes adult education centres, Jan Shikshan Nilayams and institution-based programmes.

Area-based programmes and institution-based programmes, enumerated by the 1988 guidelines can be summarized as below:

(a) Area-Based Programmes

Universities/colleges can choose from among any four subcategories under the Area-based programmes of each subcategory would comprise of a specified number of Adult Education Centres. MPFL, Continuing Education activities, community-based Population Education activities, Jana Shikshan Nilayams and Non-Formal Education Centres. Support for the JSN and NFE centres would be sought from the Government of India/State Directorates of Adult Education.

(b) Institution-based Programmes

Universities/colleges would undertake various programmes for youth on campuses such as Continuing Education, Population Education, Planning Forum, Legal literacy, Science for the People, Science and Technology for Women, Technology Transfer through Adult Education Centres, Environmental Education etc.

This guideline also speaks about organizational structure at the UGC and university level, staff development and training, learning resources, research and evaluation and also monitoring etc. In this guideline a letter from the Joint Secretary of the DOC of No. F.1-14/85 (NFE) dated 10-02-1986 regarding qualification, scales of pay of the Directors, Asst. Directors and Project Officers and other supporting staff in the departments/centres of DACEE has been reproduced. Even today this letter is referred while appointing the core faculty in the DACEE's of Indian Universities.

As to introduce institutional mechanism for post-literacy programme, the scheme of Jan Shikshan Nilayams was introduced by the Central Government in accordance with recommendation made in the National Policy of Education in 1986. The whole scheme of Jan Shikshan Nilayam is given in this guideline and also excerpts from National Literacy Mission of post-literacy and continuing education has also been annexed. In short, 1988 guideline is a milestone in the journey of the DACEEs in Indian Universities.

1992

1992 guideline is a continuation of 1988 guideline. The uniqueness of this guideline is the introduction of Nodal

Universities for DACEEs. The para related with the nodal agency university from this guideline is reproduced below for understanding its importance.

> "The monitoring of the literacy and continuing education programme of the universities/colleges would be done by the UGC through the Annual meeting convened during January-March every year for all the universities/colleges implementing the programme in that State. These monitoring meetings will be convened by the nodal university designated for individual States. A UGC representative would generally attend the meeting. In these meetings reports would be taken from each university/college implementing the literacy and/or continuing education programme in reference to the programme sanctioned to them. The nodal university would compile these reports and furnish them with their overall evaluation to the UGC in a compact form. The UGC would assist the nodal university for the expenditure incurred and for the monitoring report to be submitted to the UGC. The individual universities/colleges would pay for participation of their representatives in these meetings out of the grants sanctioned by the UGC for the programme."

Accordingly as per the provisions of nodal agency university of this guideline in 1993 the UGC had identified 13 nodal universities to coordinate and monitor the work DACEEs.

1997

UGC prepared 9th plan guideline in 1997. This is again a continuation of old guideline. This guideline directs departments to undertake adult, continuing education for university groups, adult extension education for those not eligible for university based courses and community outreach by reaching out to cater to the needs of the society.

The unique feature of this guideline is that the introduction of different type of programmes in vocational career-oriented programmes, equivalency programmes, quality of life improvement programmes, leadership and human resource development programme, social and citizenship role awareness and individual interests programmes. This guideline advises the department to develop the discipline of andragogy through academic courses and also to adopt collaborative programme approach for implementing extension education activity.

The guideline had also suggested that university authorities should create an independent faculty of non-formal education or continuing education. This policy also, speaks about the designations of the staff working in the department.

Policy of 1997 has streamlined the roles of nodal universities which include its co-ordinating role, working as documentation and dissemination of information centre, undertaking networking at different levels and also undertake advocacy activities.

As far as financial assistance to be given to the universities is concerned 1997 policy categorized universities in different phases. The phase system include nodal university, phase-III, phase-II, phase-I (A & B) departments and accordingly financial assistance was provided to the departments.

2004

In the year 2004 UGC published 10th Plan Guideline for DACEEs. This guideline carefully identified major thrusts, target groups, role and functions of DACEE, programmes and the activities, organization structure etc.

The guideline is very specific about the designations of the staff and recommended to the universities that the existing faculty working in these departments be re-designated. Director should be re-designated as Professor and Head, Assistance Director as as Reader and Project Officer be re-designated as Lecturer. This guideline encourages departments to establish.

1. Student Counseling/Placement/Guidance Centre; and
2. e-Learning Centres

In November and December 2004, UGC review committee took review of the 62 departments of adult and continuing education in the country to assess their performance. The committee under the chairmanship of Dr. D.P. Singh, former member of the Commission, interacted with Directors of different departments in the country at New Delhi (November 8 to 10, 2004) and at Chennai (December 6 to 7, 2004) and reviewed the programmes being carried out in different universities. After review of these departments the UGC had provided the financial assistance to different universities.

Present Status

The most disturbing factor in extension education in Indian Universities is the decreasing number of DACEEs. The number has come down from 103 (IXth plan) to 73 (Xth plan). The major reason for this trend is, to my mind, not taking over liability of the salary component of the staff working in these departments by the respective State Govts. Out of 73 DACEEs only 62 are reviewed by the UGC review team. Dr. Renuka Narang has prepared a brief analysis (2005) of the status of these 62 departments. Based on the facts from this report following will help us to examine the present status of the extension education in Indian universities.

1. The number of DACEEs has come from 103 (IXth plan) to 73 (Xth plan).
2. Out of 73 DACEEs only 62 are reviewed by the UGC review committee.
3. The new schemes of students counseling and e-learning are introduced during Xth plan.
4. Almost all DACEEs (barring new ones) are allotted grants to start students counselling 'centres
5. e-Learning Centres have been sanctioned to 32 DACEEs.
6. The UGC has allotted Rs. 1558.50 lakh for Xth plan period (2004-2007) to DACEEs out of which rupees 447.75 lakh is non-recurring grant.

7. 65 per cent of the Depts. had been named as Department, 32 per cent as 'Center' and 3 per cent as a 'School.'
8. As regard to full time Directors, 15 have not provided any information. 42 Directors have intimated that they are working on full time basis, but out of 42 only 24 are on clear permanent appointment and 18 are in-charge, 5 Directors are part-Directors.
9. 2000 of the core academic staff positions are vacant.
10. 44 per cent Departments conduct courses with the support of the UGC grants as well as self-supporting courses.
11. 40 per cent Departments did not conduct any workshop or seminar during 2001-2004.
12. Very few Departments have conducted state level, national level workshops/seminars.
13. 37 per cent Departments reported that they did not carry out any research work.
14. 37 per cent Departments reported that they did not carry out any research-related work.
15. 48 per cent Departments had not developed linkages with P.G. Departments, other DACEEs or with open universities.
16. 40 per cent have not developed linkages with any government body.

Concluding Remarks

As has been stated earlier decreasing number of DACEEs is disturbing trend and hence efforts are needed to be made seriously to stop this trend and again give impetus to strengthen the extension education stream. Hence, it is my humble submission, that all of us 'working in extension education should, introspect and ask a simple question that as to where we committed mistakes in nurturing this system? The observations, made by Dr. Renuka Narang, in her report entitled "A Review Study of sixty two Departments of Adult and

Continuing Education & Extension" (2001-2004), are eye-opener. For sustainable development of DACEEs concrete efforts, with scientific and systematic approach, on war-footing is need of the time. I, submit, that following would help strengthen extension education in India.

* DACEEs should be established in all Indian Universities. Keeping in view the importance of extension, the liability of the salary component of the staff of old as well as new departments be taken over by respective State Govts.
* An universities should treat the Department of Adult and Continuing Education as "Department" and should stop immediately calling these departments as "centres" or "school".
* Though the UGC guidelines from 1988 onwards recommended that core staff of DACEE be treated on par with teachers of other departments in the university that status has not been given to core staff in many universities. Efforts should be made to re-designate core staff as Professor, Reader and Lecturer. Once it happens that will help this department becoming a part of the higher education system.
* Statutory status be accorded to DACEE and for that amendments be made, if required, in the University Act and Statues of the respective university.

These are general points suggested for future development of DACEE. In addition to these, I would like to submit, following in regard to staff working at present, to introspect and for better prospects.

* Full time Directors/Heads on permanent basis be appointed in all DACEEs.
* Vacancies in the department be filled in immediately. Core Staff working in DACEE should devote sufficient time and energy in undertaking research work, particularly on community engagement areas,

along with extension education programmes. A very small amount of research work on our part has made us a pray of criticism for others working in higher education system.

* We are weak in developing linkage with other agencies. In this century for better results and sustainability it has become essential, to reduce the cost of programmes, to take help of other agencies. Therefore, it is recommended that "Partnership Approach" be adopted as modus operand.
* For making people capable of coping with problems of 21st century, efforts need to be made to make the concept of Life Long Learning a reality and that much potential is there in our system of extension education.
* Adopt flexible, adaptable, tolerant approach.
* Due attention should have to be paid towards academic programmes, governance of the system and resource mobilization for better future. Of course, quality component dominates in all walks of life.
* Blend teaching learning methods keeping in account changed educational scenario.

Please, remember we are active partners of the process of life long learning and keep in mind education is continuous process.

REFERENCES

1. The UGC guidelines on Adult and Continuing Education and Extension, 1982.
2. Report of the DOC working group on Point No.16 of the New 20 Point programme of the Government of India, 1983.
3. The DOC Guidelines on Scheme of Population Education Clubs in Universities and Colleges, 1984.
4. UGC Guidelines on Scheme of Planning Forum in universities and colleges, 1985.
5. Scheme for maximizing involvement of Students, Teachers and Institutions of Higher Education Towards Eradication of Illiteracy (MPFL) 1986.

6. New guidelines on Adult and Continuing Education and Extension Programmes in Universities and Colleges, 1988.

7. UGC Guidelines for the Programme of Literacy and Continuing Education in Universities and Colleges, 1992.

8. Guide lines for Department/Centre for Adult, Continuing Education, Extension work and field outreach, 1997.

9. Tenth Plan UGC Scheme on Adult, Continuing Education, Extension & Field Outreach) 2004.

10. S.Y. Shah, *A Source Book on Adult Education* - (Edited), Directorate of Adult Education, Govt. of India, 1989.

11. Dr. Renuka Narang, *A Review study of Sixty Two Departments of Adult and Continuing Education and Extension for the period 2001-2004*, DACEE, University of Mumbai, 2005.

10

The University Theme

Present Status, Problems and Future Directions

N. Jayakumar Rao

Prologue

As a representative of non-governmental organization participating in this seminar with laudable aims and objects, I am delighted to say that all of us must be grateful to the UGC which recognized extension as the 3rd Dimension of the Universities. It is a matter of pride for all the concerned that Sri Venkateswara University has taken up the implementation of UGC directions in all earnestness. In one of my papers presented in the same university sometime ago, I expressed my deep-felt agony that the Human resources produced by the university are not useful to the community. I took pains to detail the remedial measures to bridge the gap between the NGOs and universities. In that paper I was aiming at only a few of the University Departments which can undertake community orientation. The present chapter is to stress the need of community orientation in all the Departments in all the Universities. After all, PG level education and its products must be useful to the community, be it Economics, History, Sociology, Philosophy, Oceanography, Marine Biology or any faculty.

Bharat Still A Developing Nation

Despite 53 years of Independence we are still a Developing Nation. Nations that got Freedom much later than we did, are competing with the advanced countries. It is time that we introspect our lacunae. There are quite a few of them, but we are now pondering upon just one aspect, community-oriented University studies as a 3rd Dimension. This should have been done much earlier. But the educationists have not paid attention to it for 5 decades. But, better late than never. It is the Universities that should lift up the nation from its ever developing state.

The Universities

Universities are the wealth of the nation. Crores of rupees are spent on them. There is a treasure of knowledge in all the Departments. But all that, is primarily directed towards employment in the Govt. sector. As we are well aware of Govt. has its own problems, plus and minus points, arising out of the boons and evils that democracy brings along with it. And in the British management system that we have adopted, people with no commitment to community are elevated to high positions, the seniority criterion. Look at Korea, Japan, China, The Netherlands and the United States of America. They have grown from strength to strength. There is a lot we can learn from the Universities of those nations. Everything they do in the Universities is research oriented, community oriented, technical oriented and finally development oriented. I must be pardoned if I pass a caustic remark that what we are doing in most of our Universities is just research for research sake. The results of their research are not applied or applicable to the community. Commitment to community is deplorably lacking. But, the exercise that we have started now, is sure to yield the best fruit.

The 3rd Dimension

Extension work requires its beginning with the teaching staff and research Guides. They need to give serious thought to overhauling their educational systems. They must question themselves "Are we producing human resources that can be utilized with the governmental and non-governmental organizations, working with the communities, directing all their efforts with commitment towards the development of the community. The word "commitment" is often used without meaning it. The commitment, first of all, should be to study the evils in our society and work strenuously towards removing the evils. When our Present President Abdul Kalaam asked a group of children, who the worst enemy of our country was pat came the answer from a 12 year old girl, "poverty". In his book, "Ignited Minds", he refers to many such incidents. So she knows at least one evil. Laziness, illiteracy, superstitions, different kinds of handicaps, prostitution, no thinking on self-employment, casteism, broken families, disease, medical inadequacies, short-sighted attitudes, malnutrition, social prejudices economical differences in different classes of society, regionalism, oppression of the poor by the rich, oh! the list is endless. University human resources are aware of the theoretical part of these evils. They pass out with brilliant marks. But, when they are asked to apply their theory to uplift the community, they fail miserably. The one and only reason is that University products do not have community orientation. Hence their failure in discharging the responsibilities in the work they are entrusted with. Extension work is the only solution.

Extension—How and Where

Universities are generally situated in big cities where there will be many Governmental and Non-Governmental organizations functioning. The Universities, overcoming their framework hurdles, should tie up the human resources in their Departments with those organizations. Students in twos and threes should be deputed to work with those organizations in different sections. It could be one month in PG first year and one more month in PG second year. As far as the Research Scholars are concerned, they may work more with those organizations. Their sincerity must be supervised by a departmental cell created for the purpose. Such staff must be selected carefully testing their commitment (irrespective of recommendations and preferences). Universities must ask the students who can be called "under-trainees," to submit their reports and the reports of the supervisory staff. It is not enough if they produce a certificate from the bosses of those organizations. Thus the Governmental, quasi governmental and non-governmental organisations become laboratories of practicals for the under-trainees, just as pure sciences in laboratories.

Study material

In addition to the age-old books, study materials must be handed out, which must be prepared by the teaching staff who have knowledge of the work turned out in the Departments where the human resources are under training. The traditional thinking on working systems must undergo revolutionary changes.

The Syllabi

The 3rd Dimensional extension work must develop 3rd Dimensional textbooks. The teaching should undergo drastic changes. The teaching staff must be given reorientation in the extension work. This is a tough job but not an impossible task. The syllabus makers, at their level, should give some serious thought to awarding marks depending on the performance of the under-trainee human resources. May be, there could be an extra question paper on the 3rd Dimension. The question-paper-setters must have enough knowledge of community orientation. Only then the whole programme fructifies.

Conclusion

The present studies are more theory-oriented and are contributing to deterioration of our social structure. As one who has been associated with several Voluntary Organisations (NGOs), my experience tells me that the human resources produced by the university are not fit for consumption in our organisations. Bestow upon them exposure to practicals in NGOs, earnestly working towards the upliftment of the society and make our flag fly proudly aloft in the commity of nations. Only then our President Abdul Kalaam's vision for 2020 will be realized a reality and our Prime Minister's dreams come true.

11

Universities and Extension in the Context of Globalization

G. Lokanadha Reddy
K. Mythily

Abstract

In the present context of globalization, universities play a vital role for effective survival of mankind. As the world is shrinking in space and time, and disappearing borders, there is a growing interdependence of the people across the globe. Globalization is not just integrating the economy but also the culture, technology and governance. No country in the world, can escape from globalization in the present era and it is opening new and diverse opportunities for millions of people around the world. Universities should play an important role in the developmental process of any country keeping the global needs in mind with appropriate local actions, in terms of manpower development, research and extending scientific knowledge to the community.

In this chapter, the authors spelt out the objectives of extension by the universities and different facets of extension dimension at the university level. They explained how different Departments of Universities can extend their scientific knowledge to the community development, generation of employment for youth, extending continuing/distance education to the local communities to provide technical knowhow and so on. Likewise, the authors clearly delineated the role of universities for prevention of dreadful diseases, protection of environment, disaster management from natural and manmade calamities. They have also advocated the need for generation of global thinking skills in local communities to solve the local problems more effectively.

Globalization

Globalization is the term gaining momentum in day-to-day life of any country. In the present era, globalization has its distinctive features. The United Nations Development Program (UNDP), Human Development Report (1999) has prescribed the distinctive features of globalization as: Shrinking Space, Shrinking Time and Disappearing Borders. These features are known to be linking people's lives more profoundly, more intensively, and more immediately, than was hitherto the case. Globalization is the growing interdependence of the people across the globe, just as it is a process integrating not just the economy but culture, technology and governance. Further, globalization is opening new and diverse opportunities for millions of people around the world, including India. As India is one of the most potential economies of the world, it has to compete effectively in globalization.

When compared to 130 other countries, India ranks second in terms of population size, 103 in terms of Gross National Product (GNP), 81 in Adult Literacy, 95 in terms of Infant mortality, 84 in terms of Life Expectancy. In spite of these, it has one of the largest forces of trained and technically qualified manpower in the world. Welcome or not, its people participate in major industrial, scientific and other ventures in a large number around the world. Its people are found to learn and teach in almost every major University and Institute [both general and technical education], across the globe. And despite the incredible social, cultural and political complexities which bedevil it, India still continues to function, even if sometimes in an anarchic manner. Since Independence, the country is implementing various developmental programs through five-year plans. Eventhough, the progress is slow, we are steady in our attempt. The poverty rate is reducing year by year and the country is marching towards to stand by the side of the developed world.

On the other side of the picture, if we go by inter-sector development within the country, one can visualize the impoverished rural India on one side and the booming urban elite India on the other side. This situation leads us to go back and think our developmental programs thereby to accelerate them to meet the requirements of rural India for balanced development. As the country is having excellent trained manpower working in abundant number of colleges and universities, these institutions must be brought into the process of rural India's developmental fold. In other sense, universities should come out from the shells by tuning their academic training and research programs to cater to the needs of rural India. While, structuring the programs, these institutions should keep in mind the Globalization concepts thereby to produce more competent resources for better marketability.

Role of Universities in Extension Work

As already pointed out, the universities have to discharge adequately their responsibilities to the entire educational system and society as a whole. Extension is one of the responsibilities of higher education institutions along with major research and teaching dimensions. This is an extremely significant dimension as universities have more social responsibility.

The concept of Extension at present is not confined to extending services to the schools and colleges but also to the wider public keeping in mind the needs of the community. Any extension program must be based on the expertise of the institution, utilization of local infrastructure facilities and exploitation of manpower resources to meet the requirements of the community demands. As such, any extension program by the university must concentrate on the disadvantaged population such as women, unemployed youth, people below the poverty line, apart from people with semi- skilled and skilled to upgrade their knowledge, information and skills which result in better production of goods and services. The focus is in making the people's effective participation in developmental process.

The Objectives of Extension Activities by the Universities

1. Generation of knowledge, information and skills and pass on the same to the target population.
2. Dissemination and documentation of healthy practices in terms of training and development, so as to replicate the same in other parts of the country.
3. Sensitization of people for the effective participation in the government developmental programmes.
4. To provide on-the-job vocational training to enhance the skills of the community.
5. To understand the community problems and find out appropriate solutions through research and innovations.
6. To provide better self-employment opportunities by utilizing the government support services.
7. To train the different categories of people for sustainable development in the community.
8. To develop liaison between government departments and the public.

On the whole, the universities extension activity should start with identification of community needs to the development of appropriate training methodologies/approaches, imparting training to the personal and actual target group, generation of employment opportunities for better marketing facilities and making the people as active partners than passive spectators in the developmental programmes.

The Different Facets of Extension Dimension at University Level

As already explained in any university, extension activities have different facets. They are:

1. Universities and community development.
2. Universities and generation of employment for youth.
3. Universities and Continuing Education/Distance Education for upgrading the skills.
4. Universities and Sustainable development.

1. Universities and Community Development

Universities are higher seats of learning. The knowledge generated and created and the skills available should be useful for the betterment of the common man. This functional aspect can be achieved through University Extension activities. In other sense, bringing University to the doorsteps of the community is the need of the day. The New Educational Policy lays stress on this and expects extension to be treated as the third major component of education. The fruits of research should be made available to the community through extension activities, one following the other closely. Nowadays, interdisciplinary/multidisciplinary approach is very essential for community development. This is certainly challenging task to link extension with some disciplines like chemistry, physics, commerce, bank management, physical education and women studies and so on. The department like Adult and Continuing Education should act as a nodal center to co-ordinate the activities of various faculties of the University for developmental work in the community. The faculties with their respective programs should reach the community and in turn enrich their academic programs/curricula by incorporating the issues to solve community problems. As a nodal agency, the Center for Adult/Continuing Education should contact the developmental departments like Agriculture, Industries, Cottage and Village Industries and Voluntary Agencies, highlight the burning problems of the community. It should act as a catalyst agent. In the recent years, the new vistas of communication have been opened up for human development on account of a science and technology. Such new communication avenues should be profitably exploited for dissemination and documentation of information.

Role of Different University Department in Community Development

The Faculty of Science can organize Community Science club in villages. In organizing this, the local village talents must be exploited and it should be participatory in nature. Innovative information which will have direct bearing on the life of the community people can be discussed and demonstrated. In these science clubs, the members of the club can be trained to develop skills in them, which may improve their living conditions. These clubs can be used as potential centers for integrating the extension programs and functional training in various fields of science. These are problems of potable water, soil analysis, modern agricultural methods, identification of adulteration of food, biogas technology, horticulture, animal husbandry, sericulture, poultry etc. The Community Education Center/ Continuing Education Center must arrange for all infrastructure facilities in the villages to organize the Science Clubs and disseminate the above types of information to the rural people.

The Faculty of Human Development like Education and Women Studies can play a dominant role in the extension work of the Universities. They can impart knowledge and skills to the community about their living conditions, socio-economic development, citizenship training, gender sensitivity and so on for better quality of life. The information on ideal child rearing practices, ways and means of solving early childhood problems to prevent disabilities, helping mothers to pick up the right practices like breast feeding and weaning, right time, immunization, weight monitoring, family planning and the like.

The Faculty of Management can improve the lifestyles of the village people by giving better management practices to the community people in their day-to-day life. They can provide knowledge related to water management, banking awareness, available bank facilities consumer awareness, consumer protection and so on. The Faculty of Physical Education can give information & Training in Yoga, rural sports and stress management. A separate Rural Sports Club for village youth, can also be organized by utilizing the community education center and other infrastructural facilities in the community. Likewise, the Department/Faculty of Future Studies, Science & Technology can propagate the concepts like smokeless choolas, renewable energy from the waste (Community bio-gas plant), use of solar energy for cooking and other daily use, vermi culture for generating nutrient rich fertilizers, soil conservation, judicious use of fertilizers and pesticides, occupational hazards and ways and means of protective measure and so on.

Similarly, other departments in the Universities like Biotechnology, Geology, Home Science, and Computer Science etc can extend their knowledge to the community through appropriate ways and means. As the country is transforming rapidly towards modernization, the occupations or vocations of the people are also changing. For example, even in rural areas nowadays the youths are showing interest in Apparel and Fashion Designing, Designing Technology by using multimedia and other computer skills. As such, the universities should tune their extension activities accordingly to generate better employment opportunities to the school youth and out-of-school youth.

2. Universities and Generation of Employment for Youth

The effectiveness of any program depends on the users survivability. In other words the receiver of the program must be benefited in winning their bread and butter through the skills they acquired or provide by the university. In this respect, while organizing the training programs to the youth, women etc., it should be locale specific and employment oriented. Development of local talents by exploiting the local resources for better employability should be the principle of any training program. The following are some of the employment generation programmes for the rural and urban youth.

- Dairy Farming
- Radio and TV Repairing
- Hospitality
- Travel and Tourism
- Interior decoration
- Fire fighting
- Construction/Masonry work
- Medical Transcription
- Book keeping and Binding
- Electronics repairing
- Floral Decorations

- Freelance writing
- Photography
- Fitness and Nutrition
- Medical Office Assistant
- Fashion Designing
- Advanced vocational training programmes to the industrial workers
- Agricultural Motor repairing and rewinding
- Mushroom culture
- SCP (Single Cell Protein Productivity)
- Aquaculture
- Sea Food Production
- Preservation and Management
- Training in Kitchen gardening and Vegetable gardening
- Seedlings production
- Tailoring and Knitting and so on.

3. Universities and Continuing Education/Distance Education

The other face of extension is providing opportunities to different groups of people like industrial workers, teachers, social workers, household women and others who are in employment/semi-employment but are in need to improve their qualifications or upgrade their skills. For such population the University should offer programmes of continuing education through correspondence or distance education. While organizing these programmes, the university should keep in mind the nature and characteristics of learners, type of content and skills required to the learners, possible ways and means of adapting teaching and training technologies and continuous feedback and evaluation should be kept in mind. As such, the continuing education courses should be of 6 months, 1 year or 2 years duration leading to the award of Diplomas and Degrees.

These programmes should be ranging from development of general skills to more technical skills in the subjects like Sociology, Psychology, Management training, Personality development, Effective communicative and Persuasive skill development, Training in Enabling technologies for rural development and so on. The working governmental and non-governmental personal should be oriented about the innovative ways and means of reaching the needy people in terms of government development programmes, objectives, methodologies and benefits. Such orientation courses will have better functional value than the other. In organizing such courses, hands on experience in actual work situations should be the integral part of the programme. The knowledge generated through research should be well integrated in the training programmes and the same can be practiced in field conditions. Unless distance education programmes are tuned in these lines, it is difficult to attain the objectives of the programme.

4. Universities and Sustainable Development

Any extension programme by the University must concentrate on nation-building activities. The country is facing problems like dreadful diseases like HIV/AIDS, Degradation of Environment, Natural disasters like Earth quakes, Tsunami, Floods and Famines, Erosion of Family Values, Malnutrition and under-nutrition, Antisocial activities like terrorism and so on.

(i) *HIV/AIDS:* India is one of the worst affected country with this dreadful disease. To safeguard the present and future generations there is a greater need to sensitize the public about the safer relationships and need for family integration and value system. As universities are the potential bodies with large student manpower, they can sensitize the colleges and schools and they inturn do the same in the community and home. For this the available print and electronic media can be exploited profitably apart from traditional media.

(ii) *Degradation of Environment:* As the country is fastly moving towards modernization, urbanisation and industrialization with the exploding population, the natural resources are depleting day by day. Further, we are experiencing Air, Water, Land and Noise pollution leading to environment degradation which threaten the people to move towards low quality of life. Due to growing urbanization and industrialization the natural environmental is polluted with the factory waste, chemicals, pesticides, insecticides, radioactive waste etc., which in turn affect the sanitary conditions of the people. As a result, the quality of life is reducing. Due to deforestation, year by year we are experiencing unexpected flood and famine. To avoid this menace, the public should be educated and trained about the ways and means of sustainable development by conservation of environment. The universities should extend the supportive system to the community in the form of information, positive attitudinal building and development of technical know-how to manage their homes, community and society as a whole for sustainable development.

(iii) *Natural Disasters:* Apart from the natural disasters like floods and famine, the unexpected disasters like earthquakes and Tsunami are playing havoc in human life. In such situations people need emotional support and help. As the universities are rich in terms of knowledge, information and skills with regard to stress coping strategies and generation of material resources, they should be at the doorsteps of the people who are in need. In fact, during such crisis situations, University should coordinate the governmental and non-governmental organization activities and see that the people should be supported both materially and emotionally. Development of self-confidence and emotional guidance is the need of hour to the people in crisis situation. Within the university, the department of Adult Continuing Education and Extension should take the lead role at this end.

(iv) *Man-made Calamities:* Apart from natural disasters man made calamities like erosion of family values, malnutrition, and antisocial activities (terrorism) are playing havoc in human life. Due to erosion of family values more and more single families with single parent are existing throughout the country. As a result, children are uncared and family values and culture are far in sight year after year. Likewise, malnutrition and under-nutrition particularly in women, children and disadvantaged groups like destitute women, street children, disabled are more. Gender discrimination can be observed in every walk of life in home, community, society at large. Likewise, every part of the country is experiencing in some form or other social insecurity in the form of antisocial activities by certain vested interest group. These are the local challenges before us that are to be dealt with global views. In other sense, local problems should be dealt by understanding and developing broader perspective about the issues and purposive actions must be initiated and promoted in the public. Universities are the right bodies to generate such global thinking in the local communities to solve these burning problems locally. In other words, the concept of 'Think Globally and Act Locally' perfectly fit in to solve our problems.

12

University Extension Programmes

Problems and Perspectives

M.C. Reddeppa Reddy

Background

It was way back in 1960 that the Kothari Commission first articulated the concept of Extension and the Trinity of Teaching, Research and Extension. First time in 1977, the University Grants Commission incorporated Extension into its policy statement for Higher Education when it stated that 'the University system must assume extension as the third important responsibility and give it the same status as teaching and research'.

It was seen that the Extension Dimension was linked with National Adult Education Programme (NAEP) launched by the Government of India in 1978. UGC has provided the immediate availability of funds for setting up Cells for Adult Education in Universities. The UGC has laid the basis indirectly for life long learning and continuing education in the University system. During the first three years, i.e., 1978-1981, UGC was approved the proposal for setting up of Cells for Adult Education. These Cells have conducted Adult Education Centres (AECs) with student instructors and supervisors.

In 1982, UGC has formulated guidelines for starting of departments/centes, for adult and continuing education and extension. Further in 1983, the UGC has directed the Universities to obtain the approval of the state governments for taking over the liability of the center/department once the

UGC assistance ceased in March 1990 and also invited proposals for the establishment of a full-fledged Departments of Adult and Continuing Education and Extension before the end of VI Plan Period (by March 1985). Till 1983 the University field outreach programmes continued to be limited to literacy, post-literacy and continuing education. In 1984 the UGC introduced the Scheme of Population Education as another program to be carried out under the extension dimension. Under this scheme the Population Education Clubs (PECs) have carried out the activities both in the colleges and in the communities. Besides the population education clubs, the Planning Forums started in 1985 and broadened the horizon of the field outreach programs.

Point No. 16 of the 20 point program (1983-89) was introduced with an aim to involve the students and teachers for the eradication of illiteracy at a very rapid pace. Area Development Approach (1988) was adopted and started a number of development projects by drawing resources from other agencies including other departments of the University, government departments or NGOs. Universities and colleges also participated in the Mass Programme for Functional Literacy (MPFL, 1985) by involving youth, students, teachers, trade unions, PR Institutions, voluntary agencies and other representative organisations of people and individuals. At the instance of the National Literacy Mission (NLM) in 1992 the UGC issued a new set of guidelines pertaining to the strategies for the Total Literacy Campaign. The Universities were associated with Zilla Saksharatha Samithis and main stress was on training, professional development of the discipline, research, coordination with government and non-government organisations, etc.

Under Ninth Plan (1997-2002), the UGC continued the Adult and Continuing Education Programme in a manner that facilitated the Centers/Departments of Adult, Continuing Education and Extension to cast their own plan of action for the extension dimension specific to their own university. Attention was given in the Ninth Plan to Adult and Continuing Education for University groups that had passed the University groups that had passed the University system but had a need to return and to groups which did not have access to the University system. The Universities have a new role in the 21st century for the promotion of social change and development.

Present Status

As evidenced from the UGC's vision and strategy for the X plan, the scheme is continued to be operationalised. It is recognised that the University system should prepare the students to be the lifelong learners so as to adopt changes and learn new skills in accordance with the new demands of the world of work. The programmes and activities, which are suggested in order to cater to the needs of the different target groups are discussed hereunder.

1. Student Counselling/Career Guidance Centre

Career Guidance and High Education Counselling programmes should be organised for the benefit of the University/College students in collaboration with the commissionarates of Employment and Training, Computer Institutions, etc. The departments are expected to start student cousnelling centres to provide counselling and guidance service to students on different areas such as psychological counselling, educational career guidance, health counselling etc.

2. E-Learning

E-learning and the on-line mode for the conduct of courses be utilised for continuing education to cater to the needs of various sections of society. It allows learners to learn at their own pace, any where and any time. It covers a wide set of applications and processes including computer-based learning, web-based learning and virtual classroom. It is proposed to start a e-learning center in the selected universities to facilitate continuing education and lifelong learning for the different categories of people through distance, on-line or e-learning process.

3. Development of Academic Courses

The Departments/Centres of Adult and Continuing Education have to play a more pro-active role in developing the academic courses and offer on campus, off-campus, on-line and through e-learning. These courses should be linked specially to business and industry which would include work ethics, work culture and preparation for the changing world of work. While developing these courses, credit system should be adopted at undergraduate and post-graduate levels leading to an Associate degree in adult and continuing education for the benefit of students who are pursuing courses on the campus. The following courses are suggestive: Foundation courses, certificate, diploma, undergraduate, postgraduate, M.Phil. Ph.D. courses,—courses integrated either optional/regular with different degrees such as B.Ed., M.Ed and Professional degrees; projects related to continuing education and extension and field outreach in-built into a discipline of studies; and conduct of research particularly inter-disciplinary research for the development of theory in adult, continuing education and extension, conduct and action research/operational research.

4. Continuing Education Programmes

Continuing Education courses viz., equivalency programs, quality of life improvement programmes, income-generation programs and individual interest promotion programs are necessary for acquiring qualifications through NFE system, for facilitating improvement in the quality of life of the people for improving earnings, for promoting personality development respectively for the student youth, non-student youth and resource deprived communities. Thus the said programmes are expected to organise by the departments/centres of adult, continuing education and extension.

5. Vocational Career Oriented Courses/Programmes

The courses and programmes for people at different socio-economic and educational levels have to be organised for imparting marketable vocational skills. These courses specially focus on the demands of the changing world of work. The departments/centres are to be organised suitable vocational training programmes at the community level for the benefit of the neo-literates, unemployed youth, housewives to improve their income and to ensure better performance in their occupation. Further, it is proposed to organise vocational training programmes and apprenticeship programmes for the benefit of students in collaboration with the non-government organisations and allow them to improve their competencies and skills.

6. Extension and Field Outreach Activities

To promote a meaningful and sustained rapport between the Universities and Community, extension and field outreach activities for the deprived communities to be organised. These activities would help the faculty and students to expose to community needs, problems, issues and reaching out to socio-economic and cultural groups. Further, these activities would help to understand the major issues such as bonded labour, child labour, street children, health conditions and issues on drugs and AIDS/HIV, nutrition, sanitation, environmental issues, gender issues with stress on gender equity, human rights education, consumer rights, communal harmony and cultural integration, self-employment generation and use of technology appropriate to the society.

The work of the students involved in adult, continuing education and field outreach activities is recommended for academic credit in addition to or as a part of their regular course of studies. For determining academic credits, standards may be evolved and adopted. Each University can evolve to measures of weightage and the evaluation process for determining an academic credit.

Features of the X Plan UGC Scheme

The main features of the X plan UGC scheme are given below:

1. *Statutory status:* Accorded a statutory status to the Departments of Adult, Continuing Education and Extension with amendments, if necessary, in the University Act and Statues as that of any teaching department of the University.
2. *Unassigned grants:* The faculty of the department is also eligible for the unassigned grant of the UGC available to the University and for the research and other grants of the various UGC schemes for teachers.

3. *Special Assistance Scheme (SAP):* The existing departments are eligible for Special Assistance Programme (SAP) and other such programs of the UGC and other national/internal agencies.
4. *Advisory Committee:* Constitution of Advisory Committee and implementation committee with the Director/Head as the Convenor.
5. *Board of Studies:* To advise on the academic matters and monitor academic activities, an Academic board i.e., Board of Studies shall be constituted.
6. *Field Staff:* An additional manpower of 3 to 5 field investigators/project assistants are permitted to the Department for implementing its programmes.
7. *Hiring of Project Staff:* The miscellaneous work of the Department is to be done by outsourcing on hiring basis.
8. *Nodal Agency System:* To coordinate between the UGC and the Universities in the service area, the nodal agency system which was in vogue will be continued.
9. *New Departments:* For the establishment of a new department, UGC will release grants till the end of X plan period. To these departments, the post of one Reader and one Lecturer will be sanctioned. It is the responsibility of the concerned university to provide non-teaching staff, accommodation, furniture and other infrastructure facilities.
10. *Self-financing:* Conducting self-financing programmes/courses is essential for the sustainability of the Department.

Extension Activities Undertaken by the Department of Adult Education (SVU)

The Department of Adult Education (SVU) has undertaken the extension activities through the following centres/institutes during the last 25 years.

1. *Regional Resource Centre for Adult Education:* The Department through the Regional Resource Centre (1978-86) has provided resource support to National Adult Education Programme (NAEP) in Rayalaseema Region. The Department has organised training programmes for the government, non-governmental and university/college functionaries on different aspects of NAEP and organising literacy centres. The required material for the trainees were developed. Simple surveys and studies were also conducted in different areas of adult education.
2. *NAEP Unit:* NAEP Unit, (1982-2003) has provided technical and resource support to the colleges/ government projects and non-governmental organisations in implementing National Adult-Education by the respective implementing agenices.
3. *Nucleus Cell:* The National Literacy Mission, MHRD, Government of India has sanctioned a Nucleus Cell (1989-1991) to the Department to meet the training requirements of TLC functionaries in the University region. Training programmes were organised for field functionaries like literacy volunteers, supervisors, project officers, etc.
4. *Population Education Resource Centre (PERC):* Under UGC Population Education Resource Centre (PERC) different training programmes on population education were organised for the Principals, Lecturers and students of degree colleges in whole of Andhra Pradesh. A series of books/booklets/ modules on population education, women's equality, reproductive health etc., were brought out to disseminate the concepts of population and development education.
5. *Department of Adult Education:* The Department has organised extension programmes by adopting villages, extending technical support, strengthening of adult education movement, bringing out an half-

yearly journal, creating awareness on different national/international days of importance as described hereunder:

Adoption of villages: The Department was adopted Chandamamapalle (Tribal Habitation, 2002-03) and Lakshmicheruvu village (2003-04) and organised adult education and development programmes.

Technical support: The department has extended technical support in preparation teaching/learning materials, organising training/orientation programmes, monitoring and evaluation, implementing a new project called an innovative method of teaching literacy through play way method under the concept of joy of learning to the implementing agencies viz., Zilla Saksharatha Smithies of Chittoor, Kadapa and Nellore districts.

Strengthening of Adult Education Movement

1. *Hosting the branches of National Bodies:* The department is strengthening the adult education movement in cooperation with Indian Adult Education Association (IAEA), New Delhi and All India Council for Mass Education and Development (AICMED), Kolkata by way of starting Andhra Pradesh Branch of IAEA and South Zone of AICMED and organising different programmes.
2. *Journal of Adult Education and Extension:* The department is bringing out half-yearly Journal of Adult Education, Extension with an aim to strengthen the discipline and National Literacy Mission by way of disseminating the research findings, innovations, experiences and sharing of views.
3. *Celebration of National / Internal Days of importance:* The Department has been organising important National/Internal Days viz., Internal Literacy Days (Sept. 8), Internal Women's Day (March 8), Education Day (Nov. 11), World AIDS Day (Dec. 1st), National

Science Day (Feb. 28th), etc. with an aim to create awareness among the rural people on literacy, gender equality, health, science, etc.

Further the department has undertaken students' projects, research projects and evaluation studies as shown below:

(a) *Students' Projects:* Projects were assigned to the students to carryout in the rural communities as a part of fulfilment of the requirements of curriculum. They have completed various projects under the supervision of the faculty. The projects were evaluated and marks were awarded.

(b) *Research Projects:* A number of major and minor research projects were undertaken by the faculty members with the financial support from the different funding agencies viz., UGC, ICSSR, NCERT, MHRD, Ministry of Tribal Affairs, Department of Women and Child Development, Planning Commission etc. and the reports were submitted to the respective funding agencies.

(c) *Evaluation studies:* The department has also conducted evaluation studies to evaluate literacy programme in Chitradurga district of Karnataka, Akshara Sankranti of Prakasam district in Andhra Pradesh and Jana Shikshana Sansthans of Thrissur, Kottayam (Kerala) and Ramananthapuram (Tamil Nadu) with the financial support of NLM. Open schools in Chittoor district of Andhra Pradesh were also evaluated.

Recently the department has organised career guidance and higher education counselling programs in the month of October 2005 and covered 850 undergraduate and graduate students. Later, the department has organised trainers training programme on the same theme for the selected lecturers of the affiliated colleges in Chittoor district. Further career exhibition are also organised in collaboration with the Commissionarate of Employment and Training, Government of Andhra Pradesh, Hyderabad in different places viz., Tirupati, Puttur and Nagari.

Problems in Conducting Extension Activities

With regard to implementation of the MPFL, UGC has observed certain difficulties/problems:

(i) Reports both initial and terminal of the programme were not sent properly and in time;

(ii) Proper evaluation of the learners was not done and results of literacy attainment were not made available to the UGC.

(iii) Reports regarding involvement of students, enrolment of learners and evaluation were not compiled at University level and forwarded to the commission in time;

(iv) Lack of coordination between the NSS programme coordinators and the department/centre of adult, continuing education and extension in the University.

(v) The Universities were not able to meet the targets communicated to them for involvement of students.

There are specific problems in implementing adult education programmes in the University sector (Reddy MCR, 1988) They are:

1. Lack of awareness among the University functionaries viz., Principals, teachers and students on the seriousness of the problem of illiteracy.
2. Difficulty in ensuring support from faculty members.
3. Non-availability of funds for travel expenses, material production, exhibition, publicity, etc., under the scheme.
4. Delays in sanctioning funds and programmes by insisting on routing all proposals through the Registrar.
5. Non-availability of teaching/learning materials on time for use in the centres.
6. Lack of availability of students and supervisors throughout the year.

7. Lack of intensive training and orientation of instructors.
8. Lack of coordination among the various agencies involved in the programme.
9. Lack of supporting staff in the colleges.

The department has implemented the Chandamammapalle (Tribal Habitation) Literacy Project (2002-03) with an aim to serve the deprived community and to enable the students to gain practical experiences. The project was carried out with the faculty, research scholars and PG students. The University students were acted as volunteers in the centres at least two days in a week. Arrangements were made with local volunteers to run the centres on the other days of the week. The project was organised from October 2002 to April 2003. While carrying out the project, the department/organisers have faced certain problems (MCRR, 2003). They are given below:

1. *Lack of extension-connected infrastructure facilities* such as vehicle fitted with public - address system, mobile tent, mobile telephone, film projector for easy access and for attracting wider community.
2. *Lack of community support* particularly from the local elders, youth and women due to traditional beliefs, social inhibitions, poor attitudinal change etc. Even the panchayat raj personnel could not extend their help and support due to the pressure of work and priorities;
3. *Low participation of Enrolled learners:* Though the learners have shown interest to attend the centres initially, they could not participate in the centers effectively in the specified timings due to poor commitment, the nature of work they involved, preparation of food and feeding of children, tiredness after hard labour, continuous prolonged illness etc.
4. *Lack of proper accommodation:* Due to non-availability of proper accommodation, centers were organised under the street lights. The centres could

not function properly particularly during the rainy and winter seasons and time and again the student volunteers have returned to the campus with much disappointment.

5. *Irregular attendance of student/local volunteers:* Though proper arrangements have been made for batching and matching of student volunteers and the learners, the students could not attend the centers on the scheduled days due to prolonged absence in the classes, poor commitment for social service, low competencies and inconsistent priorities. The local volunteers have not organised the centres during the non-scheduled days due to their under-age, maturity of mind, poor organisational skills, etc.
6. *Constraints of official timings and work load:* As any other department the faculty in the department are attending to their class work and fulfilling their workload. While organising the extension activities, they have to work extra hours and face lot of inconvenience in planning, preparation and execution in the rural and deprived communities at distance places.
7. *Lack of financial support:* Though the service is done on voluntary basis, the extension activities require sufficient budget for meeting certain basic minimum needs such as refreshments, travel, contingencies, publicity cost, follow-up measures, etc.

Perspectives

In order to widen the scope of extensive activities in the University system the following to be taken into consideration:

1. *Link with Business and Society:* The Adult and Continuing Education and Extension as an important element, needs to be further widened by reorienting it as link with business and society. In the changed economic environment outreach activities in lifelong education in aspects related to skills, wealth,

environment, physical fitness, values, good citizenship and such other factors which lead to good life, attain special importance.

2. *Involvement of other departments in the extension activities:* Besides the departments of adult, continuing education and extension, the other departments in the universities such as Education, Home Science, Population Education, Sociology, Anthropology, Zoology, Bio-chemistry, Geology, Law, Library Science, Communication and Journalism etc. have much to do for the community in disseminating information on different aspects. Now, knowledge in the fields is fast changing from time to time and the society must be kept abreast with the latest knowledge through various extension lectures demonstrations, workshops, simple and short duration programmes, vocational education, on the job training. These departments should also take initiation to organise extension programmes either independently or collaboratively. But, these departments should receive grants for the extension programmes from the UGC.

3. *Catalytic Role of Adult Education Departments:* The departments of Adult on Continuing Education and Extension should take lead in motivation, mobilisation and coordination of the extension activities of the other departments in the Universities. These departments are nodal centers to conduct extension, community work and developmental programmes.

4. *Privilege Leave:* Since the nature of extension departments demands that they should be available beyond working hours and throughout the year, they be given privilege leave and encashment of earned leave.

5. *Project Work:* Project work should be made compulsory in all the departments so as to work in

the social environment by the students either individually or in groups. The work of the students can be evaluated and marks be awarded.

6. *Curricular Adjustments:* Curriculum should be modified and integrate with the development activities in the community. Integration of curriculum with the community service is possible by introducing a compulsory 100 marks paper at the first degree level. Performance in the community work should be given weightage for admission to higher degree and for employment, extension should be integrated into the UG foundation courses, applied and core courses etc.

13

Value Education Through Extension Activities

T. Kumaraswamy
G. Hussain Reddy
K.G. Bharathi

Today, there is erosion of values at all levels about which all of us have to bother about. Violence, robbery, crime, corruption, untouchability, environmental degradation, communal violence, adulteration, lack of belief in others, lack of respect to elders and teachers etc., have become rampant. We are missing with the following things in general.

1. Basic needs (proper food, housing, drinking water and good environment);
2. Social needs (responsible parents, brothers and sister, socialisation, freedom to live and lead the life, social justice, people's participation in Government programmes and political commitment);
3. Economic needs (economic security, employment, equal distribution of wealth, ability to fight for fundamental human rights);
4. Quality of life-oriented needs (Happiness, joy, devotion, peace, satisfaction, patience, commitment, humbleness and sincerity).

All the above aspects are the concern of value education. Without values, a nation perishes and it is through value education we will be able to maintain harmony and development of the society. Universities as on centres of excellence and higher learning have a major role to play in imparting value education to the illiterate and downtrodden sections of the society. Values are described as the socially defined desires and goals that are internalised through the process of conditioning, learning and socialisation. Values are related to what we want to become and what we desire to be.

Values can be classified as follows:

(a) Religious Value

This value is defined in terms of faith in God, attempt to understand him, fear of divine wrath and acting according to the ethical codes prescribed in the religious books. The outward acts of behaviour expressive of this value are going on pilgrimage, living a simple life, having faith in the religious leaders, worshipping God and speaking the truth.

(b) Social Value

This value is defined in terms of charity, kindness, love and sympathy for the people, efforts to serve God through the service of mankind, sacrificing personal comforts and gains to relieve the needy and the afflicted of their misery.

(c) Democratic Value

This value is characterized by respect for individually, absence of discrimination among persons on the bases of sex, language, religion, caste, colour, race and family status, ensuring equal social, political and religious rights to all, impartiality and social justice and respect for the democratic institutions.

(d) Aesthetic Value

Aesthetic value is characterized by appreciation of beauty, love for fine arts, drawing, painting, music, dance, sculpture, poetry and architecture, love for literature, love for decoration of the home and the surroundings, neatness and systematisation in the arrangement of the things.

(e) Economic Value

This value stands for desire for money and materials gains. A man with high economic value is guided by considerations of money and material gain in the choice of his job. His attitude towards the rich persons and the industrialists is favourable and he considers them helpful for the progress of the country.

(f) Knowledge Value

This value stands for love of knowledge of theoretical principles of any activity, and love of discovery of truth. A man with knowledge value considers the knowledge of theoretical principles underlying a work essential for success in it. He values hard work in studies, only if it helps to develop ability to find out new facts and relationships, and aspires to be known as the seeker of knowledge. For him knowledge is virtue.

(g) Hedonistic Value

Hedonistic value, as defined here, is the conception of the desirability of loving pleasure and avoiding pain. For a hedonist, the present is more important than the future. A man with hedonist value indulges in pleasures of senses and avoids pain.

(h) Power Value

The power value is defined as the conception of desirability of ruling over others and also of leading others. The characteristics of a person high power value are that he prefers a job where he gets opportunity to exercise authority over others, that he prefers to rule in a small place rather than serve in a big place, that the fear of law of the country rather than the fear of God deters him from having resources to unapproved means for making money, and that he is deeply status conscious and can even tell a lie for maintaining the prestige of his position.

(i) Family Prestige Value

The family prestige value is the conception of the desirability of such items of behaviour, roles, functions and relationships as would become one's family status. It implies respect for roles which are traditionally characteristic of different castes of the Indian society. It also implies the maintenance of the purity of family blood by avoiding inter-caste marriages. It is respect for the conservative outlook as enshrined in the traditional institution of family.

(j) Health Value

Health value is the consideration of keeping the body in a fit state for carrying out one's normal duties and functions. It also implies the consideration for self-preservation. A man with high health value considers good physical health as essential for the development and use of his abilities.

Rama Murthi Commission (1990) observes 'Education must provide a climate for the nurture of values, both as a personalised set of values, forming one's character and including necessary social, cultural and national values so as to have a context and meaning for actions and decisions and in order to enable the persons to act with conviction and commitment. Students at graduate and post-graduate levels should do extension work as part of NSS and NCC. The mottos of 'Study and Serve', 'Each One Teach One', 'Adoption of Villages by the University and Colleges' will get a meaning through such efforts. Dramas, role play, lecture, discussion, kalajathas, songs, open air theatre, film shows, personal contacts can be utilised in extending the activities. The values of team work, democratic outlook, social justice, knowledge and community living can be improved among students through their participation in extension. The works can be allotted to students depending upon their knowledge, interests and abilities.

Organising value education activities by the students and staff members is not an easy thing and it requires a scientific approach to the issue and co-ordinating skills. How to make value education activities participatory at the grassroot level? When, how and where to conduct the programmes? What resources are needed and how to follow up the activities? are a few questions in this regard.

The following are different areas on which attention is needed.

NATIONAL AND LOCAL PROBLEMS

This activity comprises of identifying the topics for discussion, collection of information, informing the participants, organising the discussion, follow-up and remedial action. It is not so easy to conduct the discussion at the village level on value education by involving the community. This requires proper training and orientation. A wide range of topics of national interest like national integration, drinking water, sanitation, dairy, agriculture, population, education, environment, patriotism, women's emancipation, child labour, health aspects and local issues like untouchability, superstitions, equal wages, land development can be taken up for discussion at the central level.

(a) Population Explosion

Population growth leads to disruption in income distribution and exacerbates tensions. Additional resource mobilisation in severely affected. A fast growth of population outstrips the rate of economic growth leading to unhealthy competition for limited opportunities. People are forced to accept lowly paid jobs and the opportunity cost of labour steeply goes down. Huge sections of population are left behind and outside the modern technological culture. Thus, the single phenomenon of population explosion can totally disrupt the social fibre of a developing country. This must be clearly brought home to the masses.

(b) Environment

A direct result of population explosion is degradation of environment and ecology. Loss of forests and green pastures, destruction of watersheds, soil erosion, floods, droughts, etc., affect the natural environment and ecology to the great detriment of the human population. Along with environmental and ecological degradation, population also creates problems of pollution which again works to the great detriment of the human race. There has been more than 300 time increase in the motor vehicles after the second World War and air pollution has become a serious problem in almost all the leading cities of India. Lesson in preservation of environment and ecology and avoiding pollution are a necessary part of the proposed course curricula.

(c) Patriotism

There is an imminent need to inculcate a sense of patriotism in the group of people mentioned above and who pose a great threat to the sovereignty and integrity of this country. There are many who do not know what national anthem is, what is the significance of the national flag, what are the national heritage and culture. Without pride and faith in one's own country, there can hardly be any hope of sacrifice for its welfare and growth.

(d) National Integration

No other country in the world has suffered more severe damage than Indian on account of communal riots, inter-religious hatred, regionalism, linguistic quarrels, caste and sub-caste tensions, etc. Persons and parties in power have often exploited these discordant elements of the society. If the masses are made to understand the true meaning of national integration and communal harmony they would not be such an easy prey to the ill designs of the vested interests. The masses need to be properly educated in these aspects.

(e) Atrocities on Weaker Sections

Atrocities on the weaker sections of the society like the Scheduled Castes, Scheduled Tribes and other Backward Castes have become so common that even the knowledgeable and the educated have accepted them as a part of life. Same is more or less true in regard to the atrocities on women and abuse of the children.

(f) Social Evils

Social evils like nepotism, corruption, indiscipline, lack of a will or preparedness for hard work, dishonesty, etc., are spreading in almost all sections of the society. This is perhaps because there are no ideals of good moral behaviour before the masses. What is disgusting is the indifference of those in power, whether social, economic or political towards these social evils. The Indian philosophy of simplicity and sacrifice can now be found only in the old library books. Greed for money, and more money, has become the order of the day. Clearly this is the result of want of a good moral education system.

(g) Games and Sports Activities

Sports and games lead to physical strength, psychological freeness, social movement and longevity. Games and sports activities like Kabbadi (indigenous game), kho kho, carroms, chess, cricket, volley ball, badminton, tenny coit, running race etc., can be organise to promote health value.

(h) Education for All

Recognising the importance of literacy the Government of India is emphasising upon universal enrolment and retention at primary levels and is taking steps to provide basic literacy to the illiterate adults in the shortest possible time. Students and staff members can motivate the poor and illiterate people to send their children to schools, secure co-operation of village education committee members and elders to check school dropouts and leftovers and motivate the illiterates and semi-literates to attend the literacy and continuing education.

The role of parents in primary education needs to be highlighted. The principles bringing up children in a family are: Treat all the children with equal affection; Make their friends welcome in your home; Do not quarrel in front of them; Be truthful to each other; Never lie to them; Always answer their queries; Do not punish them in the presence of others; Be constant in your moods and affection, Keep nearer to them; Concentrate on their good points and not failures. The best inheritance that a parent can give a child is spending at least ten minutes of his time in the academic progress which will acts a stimulus to the child. Parents should be educated first and they should be motivated to participate in the parent-teacher associations and school functions.

(i) Celebration of Important Days

The students and staff members can celebrate important days like International Literacy Day, Independence Day, World Population Day etc., at the continuing education centre. The prerak can explain the importance of the day by conducting meetings, rallies, etc., by involving the resource persons so that the message reaches the public more effectively. The list of the days that can be celebrated by the prerak is as follows:

— January 12: National Youth Day;
— January 26: Republic Day;
— February 28: National Science Day;
— March 8: International Women's Day;
— March 15: World Consumer Rights Day;
— March 22: World Day for Water;
— April 7: World Health Day;
— April 22: World Earth Day;
— May 1: Workers/Labour Day;
— May 19: World Telecommunication Day;
— May 31: Anti-Tobacco Day;
— June 5: World Environment Day;
— June 11: World Population Day;
— August 15: Independence Day;
— September 5: Teachers Day;
— September 8: World Literacy Day;
— September 16: World Ozone Day;
— October 1: International Day for the Elderly;
— October 2: Gandhi Jayanti;
— October 4: World Animal Welfare Day;
— October 16: World Food Day;
— November 14: Children's Day;
— December 1: World AIDS Day;
— December 10: Human Rights Day; and
— December 23: Farmers Day at the community level.

The list is only suggestive but not exhaustive.

(j) Programmes to promote Mental Peace

The need of the hour to mankind today is value education which touches upon mental peace, happiness, sincerity, morality, social understanding, patriotism, culture, standard of life, etc.

Adult learners attending the continuing education centres are confronted with different problems in the society. They are in need of programmes to promote peace, happiness, etc., among them.

The universities and colleges should have an understanding about the local concerns, local agencies working for the well being of the poor and downtrodden societies, cultural and spiritual agencies, philanthropists etc., for taking their co-operation in conducting the value based extension activities at the grassroot level. If the universities discharge their duties adequately and properly then they are well with the nation and people. Let value education activities herald, symbolise and contribute to new development strategies.

REFERENCES

1. Chittibabu, S.V. (1987), Value Orientation in Higher Education, *University News*, Vol. XXV, No. 42, October 19.
2. Kapur, J.N. (1995), Transmission of Values through Higher Education System, *University News*, February 24.
3. Kar, N.N. (1996). *Value Education: A Philosophical Study*, Associated Publishers, Ambala Cantt.
4. Kurup, M.R., Matte, C.R. (1998), Higher Education in a Developing Society, *University News*, Vol. 36, No. 24, June 15, pp. 48-53.
5. *National Educational Policy* (1986), Ministry of Human Resource Development, Government of India, New Delhi.
6. Sarma, A.P. (1995), Values are permeated, *University News*, December 11.
7. Seshadri et al., (1992), *Education in Values—A Source Book*, NCERT.
8. Venkataiah, N. (1998), *Value Education*, A.P.H. Publishing Corporation, New Delhi.

14

Extension as the Third Dimension of the Universities

Present Status, Problems and Future Directions

K. Rathnaiah
R. Sampoorna
M.R. Gowramma

India is a vast country with her roots in villages. More than eighty per cent of her population live in the rural areas. Therefore, a veritable truth follows that her development is the development of rural areas. India is the biggest democratic country in the world in terms of her population which is the second largest next to China. Hers a complex society with an admixture of umpteen castes and sub-castes and diverse religions and linguistic groups. Consequently her problems such as illiteracy, unemployment, malnutrition, poverty and disease, etc., are concentrated in the rural areas. As the World Bank estimates that three-fourths of people are in absolute poverty and they are in the developing countries of Asia which reflect the level of per capita income, hunger, poverty and deprivation in the rural areas. Although, India has made some appreciable and good strides in Science and technology and investments has been increased in the successive plan periods, hundreds of millions of people in the rural areas are caught up in abject, degrading and most inhuman conditions like poverty, malnutrition, disease, illiteracy and unemployment.

Though it is imperative for the government to reorient the development policies in order to assail directly the personal poverty. It is also essential that the education has to play a predominant role in correcting the serious imbalances that have resulted any needful and constructive implementation of educational policies particularly at the rural level. It will create more awareness among the people which will help them to be self-sufficient. It has been already stressed that the national development of India depends on the development of rural areas. This can be effectively brought out through education. Education may be formal and non-formal. Formal education deals with the regular education i.e., confined to Schools, Colleges and Universities. This form of education serves the interests of only some people. Since large segment of population constitutes illiterates and dwell in rural areas where they are constantly engaged in agricultural operations. It is therefore essential to have non-formal education for those who can not attend the Colleges and Universities.

Extension is not also a concept or an idea but also a practical application and extension of simple education which is stretched into villages for the benefit of the deprived and disadvantageous people who are illiterates and neo-illiterates. It signifies an out of school system of education for adults and youth. Extension education has increasingly becoming popular in the developing countries where majority of people are illiterates and reeling under abject poverty and economic backwardness. It deals with creation, transmission and application of knowledge of people with a view to help them live better by learning ways of improving their family living, their farms and enterprises.

Non-formal Extension Education has many advantages for the developing countries like India. It brings desirable and constructive changes in the knowledge, attitude and skills of rural people. It helps people help themselves. It is kind of education by which learning is done by doing. It brings scientific information to village people and takes them to the scientific institutions. It is a continuous educational process in which people in the villages learn new things in their day-to-day life. Extension has gained importance in the recent times as the need is obvious especially for the rural economy with its major component of agriculture. In other words, through the extension and service approach rural people are stimulated to make changes that result in more efficient production and marketing of farm products, more comfortable homes, improved health and more satisfying family and community life. It assists people to discover and analyse their problems, their felt and unfelt needs, develops leadership qualities among people and help them in organising groups to solve their problems and disseminate information based on research and practical experience in such a manner that people would accept it and put it into actual practice.

Extension as the Third Dimension of the Universities

The aim of the chapter is confined to the usefulness of extension for rural development this is the third dimension of the Universities in fact teaching and research are the first and second dimensions at the Universities. You can not apply yesterday's methods today and be in business tomorrow is a maximum which applies as much to the economy of a nation as to the business conduct of any group or individual. The need is very obvious especially for the rural economy with its major component of agriculture. The rural people should know and adopt useful research findings from time to time and also transmit their problems to the research workers of the universities for solution. The researchers neither have the time nor are they equipped for the job of persuading the villagers to adopt scientific methods and to ascertain from them about the rural problems. On the other hand, it is impracticable for the millions of farmers to visit the research stations and learn things by themselves. Thus an agency is required to bridge the gulf between the research workers and the people at large to play the dual role of interpreting the results of research, i.e., Universities to the farmers as well as of conveying the farmer's problems to the research stations for solution. This agency is termed 'Extension' and the personnel manning this agency or organisation or University are called 'extension workers'. To equip the prospective extension workers for their job, it is necessary for them to be trained adequately in the formal teaching universities.

The other aspect of the chapter is confined to the effective use of Audio-Visual Aids in Extension Education. An Audio-Visual Aid is an instructional device in which the message can be heard as well as seen. People learn through seeing, hearing and doing; looking, listening and acting. Audio-Visual Aids offer the teacher/investigator unique opportunities to increase the effectiveness and clarity of the ideas being transferred. They enable learners to see, hear, look and listen more clearly, more fully and with greater understanding insight. The Audio Aids include radio, recordings, tape, disc, wire and sound commentaries in public address system. The Visual-Aids may be projected or non-Projected. The Projected Visual Aids are Charts, Posters, Chalk boards, flash cards, photographs, etc. The non-projected Visual Aids are slides, motion pictures, illustrations projected through opeidoscope and overhead projector. The present status of the extension departments in the Universities are no longer using the Audio-Visual Aids. The success and effective implementation of extension programmes at University level depend upon various factors. Villages adopted for carrying out demonstrations or anything must be in proximity near to the scientific institutions. The cooperation of schools, village officials and NGOs in the villages must be sought. If necessary door-to-door campaign must be done at the first instance before the programmes are undertaken. This is only to create a congenial atmosphere and right understanding in the people. The local leadership must be fully utilised. If the villages indicate positive results and highly challenging the teacher/investigator must proceed with the programmes with more zeal and innovative spirit to effect more dramatic changes in the day-to-day living.

Suggestions

1. Extension Programmes must be incorporated in the curriculum in all the departments at University level and it should be made compulsory.
2. Two day week must be allotted for Extension work.
3. Each and every department must be provided Audio-Visual Aids.

15

Extension as the Third Dimension of the University

Present Status and Future Directions

K. Sudha Rani
G. Hussain Reddy

The Indian socio-economic scene has been witnessing numerous changes in the last fifty years. These changes, besides others, also affected the system of education, service providers, curriculum and approaches towards human resource development. The expansion of knowledge has accelerated in today's time and generating a gap between various segments of the population because of differential access. More and more people are being called upon to assimilate an increasing volume of information, acquire new skills for employment, use of leisure time, realise their potential, and develop attitude conducive to their participation in the process of the development. The institution of higher education, though not being in sensitive to these socio-economic changes began to either strengthen their effort and resolve or initiate the process of meeting these challenges by devising ways, which were necessarily not in consonance with the requirements and traditions of higher education institution, which could meet the rising aspirations, personal expectations, technological advances, increase in information's and growing awareness of conditions of economically and educationally disadvantaged groups as well as others at the various level of growth and development. Thus emerged the concept of extension in higher education. Extension as the third dimension in university implies that the resources and knowledge available with the university is made available to the people in order to improve their knowledge skills and economic status and also enable the university community comprising of students, teachers, researchers and others to develop an insight into the problems faced by the community through extension system of the university. UGC in India articulated the idea of extension in 1977 and 1982 and called for the introduction of extension as a third but equally important function of the system of higher education.

Objectives of University Extension to the Community

- To help the rural masses to appreciate the opportunities, duties and privileges of living in an organised way.
- To raise the whole standard of rural life by promoting social, cultural and intellectual activities in the villages.
- To bring to the rural people the prevailing knowledge and technological advances.

Present Status of the extension activities of the Universities

It has become increasingly evident that university in developing countries are accepted as instruments of change charged with the mandate to produce trained manpower, the education of good citizens, and as centres for the advancement and accumulation of knowledge. As an instrument of change, a university pursues knowledge for the service of society and the spirit inculcated into teaching research and outreach or extension functions. At present only very few social science departments like adult education, population education sociology and home science in the university are involved in the extension work. The expertise and academic excellence of the other faculties of the universities are not reaching to the community thus creating a lacunae. In the universities the emphasis is on the teaching and research and has been neglecting the extension.

Problems

Absence of pre-set outreach goals: A clear set of outreach goals will be useful to a university so that it can allocate its resources accordingly. With these goals clearly identified, the university can identify the transformations it must take in order to achieve the future goals. At present no pre-set goals of extension activities in the Universities was observed.

Inadequate financial allocation: The university will have to judiciously manage and allocate its financial resources for its various functions. Investments in equipment, sizeable operating budget are necessary and is lacking.

Lack of staff commitment: In order to conduct outreach activities effectively, a university really needs to maximise the effective use of faculty time and expertise. Lack of commitment among the staff is becoming a serious road block in conducting extension activities.

Absence of internal linkages: The expertise and academic talents of a university will be found in the various academic departments. It is necessary to establish viable linkages with these academic departments that are effectively coordinated to support the outreach activities. Absence of the linkages may lead to duplication or may fail in providing the sufficient information to the rural masses.

Future Directions

Keeping in view the role of university in extension and field outreach activities the author proposed the directions to be followed in future are presented in three aspects namely, (A) Administrative structure, (B) Involvement of different disciplines in extension activities and (C) Linkages with other agencies involved in community development.

I. Administrative Structure

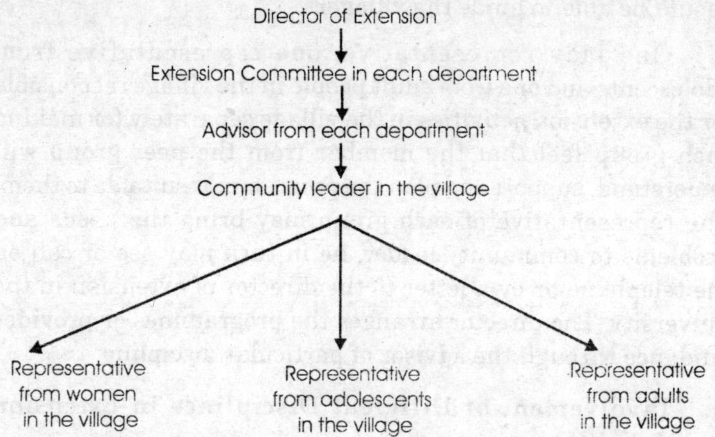

There should be a director at the university level to look after the entire responsibility of the extension work, to co-ordinate the extension work of different disciplines and to organise extension activities depending upon the needs of the community. An extension committee should be formed in each department and are responsible to plan and organise the extension activities. An advisor or the leader of the extension committee from each department has to play an important role in order to provide the community with information and direction according to the needs and requirements of the community. He is to be well informed about the latest development in the respective discipline. He is to be responsible for making the villagers feel that he is a real partner in village affairs and should make his help and co-operation needed and valued in every village activity. Advisor from each faculty with the help of the students will kept close contact with the community leader of the village will plan and organize the programmes in the villages.

Community leader should be the local person and he should be found to touch upon all aspects of rural life. He should have comprehensive understanding of the village people and their problems. He has to take the problems to the advisor and should act as a liaison between the community and advisor and should be able to guide the villagers.

One lady representative, one representative from adolescents and one from adult people in the village responsible for the extension activities in the village separately for making each group feel that the member from the peer group will understand, support and plan the programmes suitable to them. The representative of each group may bring the needs and problems to community leader, he in turn may see or call on the telephone or by a letter to the director of extension in the university. The director arranges the programmes or provides guidance through the advisor of particular discipline.

II. Involvement of Different Disciplines in Extension Activities

It is important to recognise that the university extension services to the community have not been associated exclusively with any one of the social science disciplines. The extension activities of various disciplines of the university are important. Due to lack of knowledge about the other disciplines the author has suggested the roles of few disciplines briefly as follows:

Sociology: It is a science deals with basic knowledge of the society—its demographic constitution, equipped with conceptual and theoretical framework, methodological tools to study and understand society and essential to find out the real conditions of the community.

Home Science: Home science is largely conceived of as "a field of knowledge and service primarily concerned with strengthening family life. Home science department through extension activities can help in training women to take care of home, family, child, cooking, improving the services and goods used by families, nutritional needs, the selection, preservation, preparation and use of food, clothing and textiles etc.

Psychology: Psychology deals with the mental health of the people. Mental health is the capacity of an individual to form harmonious adjustments to his social and physical environment. It is high time that the psychology department of the university to involve in rural development activities such as bringing up awareness about mental health, educating them about the mental illness, causative factors treatment and about the institutions which take care of various types of mental disorders.

Education: In the rural area, the department of education in the university can play the roles such as:

- Identification of drop-outs from the formal schools and knowing reasons for their drop-out.
- Encouraging the drop-outs to continue their education through non-formal education.
- Conducting in service training programmes to non-formal and open school teachers.
- Providing educational and occupational information to the rural people through guidance programmes.

Population Education: Population Education is one of the major talking points of today due to population problems. The department can undertake population awareness programmes. They include providing knowledge on dangers of population growth, about nutrition, health, family planning, sex education, etc.

Political Science: The discipline of political science has considerable potential for undertaking extension activities and some of the areas in which the awareness among the rural masses should be developed by this discipline are, ideas and ideologies of political parties, knowledge of constitution, political set-up at the central, state and district level, importance of democracy, elections, voting and participation of the village people in different development communities etc.

Zoology: Zoology is a science deals with animals. Though each and every animal has its own importance in nature but a few of them, such as some mammals, birds, fishes, prawns, and insects like silk worm, honey bee etc. are gaining too much importance. These animals have a very good status in small scale industries, by which socio-economic status of the nation can be raised. Since the faculty members of the zoology department have necessary expertise in the above fields, their services can be best used in helping the rural poor in establishing aquaculture, sericulture, fish culture, poultry etc.

Bio-technology: The faculty of bio-technology can develop awareness among the rural masses about the bio-pesticides, bio-fertilisers and their importance.

Environmental Science and Chemistry: Man is continuously exposed to the environmental pollutants like, industrial chemicals, food additives, ionizing radiation. The negative effects of these chemicals have become pronounced in the last few years. Suitable educational programmes focusing on specific signs and symptoms of toxicity in association with specific chemical should be organised by the faculty in rural areas to create awareness among them.

Economics: From this department the extension services may be provided in studying the economic conditions prevailing in the community, organising awareness programmes on government policies, programmes and welfare measures for the development of poor, etc.

Commerce: This discipline can extend their activities to the rural areas by providing information on banks, industries, public and private enterprises in business, developing leadership skills, savings, investments etc.

Law: The awareness on different laws for the protection of the people among the masses, legal advisory and consultancy services to the people can be provided by this department.

Botany: The people from this faculty can help the rural communities in guiding them on soil conservation, vegetables and fruits cultivation, medical plants, pests and weed control, and improved practices of farming etc.

Journalism: The department of journalism can help all of the other disciplines in the preparation and publication of news letter, posters, slides, charts and electronic devices according to the requirements of different disciplines of the university to use in the rural areas.

III. Support to Other Organisations

The university found consciously and constructively to relate its activities to integrated development by being responsible to national and specific community needs. On the other hand NGOs and development agencies of the government work for the people, implementing the programmes and contributing for the human resources development. The university has to give support to these agencies in the following way:

A. *Piloting of new strategies and approaches:* The university can provide support to plan and carryout the pilot project on new strategies and approaches.

B. *Training:* Many NGOs and government agencies may have their own training programmes. However, they may not be able to cover all aspects or all levels of their personnel. This is where the university can helpful in the gap by complementing the training programme that it can best provide.

C. *Production of support materials:* Another major support that the university can provide is the creation and production of support material that have the knowledge bases in the academic disciplines of the university. Many implementing agencies do not have the necessary resources to sustain this creative activity, that has to be depend on new ideas and findings.

Conclusions

The university is found consciously and constructively to relate its activities to integrated development by being responsible to national and specific community needs. The task of integrated development is a multifaceted one which requires multi-disciplinary approach. To attain the integrated development of the rural communities and in order to conduct outreach activities effectively, the expertise and academic talents of all of the disciplines in the university should be extended and their involvement is very essential.

16

Extension as Third Dimension in the University System

Certain Issues and Possibilities

V. Reghu

According to UGC X plan guidelines "Extension" is seen as the third dimension equal in importance to teaching and research. It is the result of growing realization that the Universities and Colleges having institutional resources have an obligation to involve in the development process of the community. As visualized earlier by UGC all Universities are expected to establish a Department for institutionalizing "Extension" with a view to meet the current needs and demands of adult and continuing education in their respective areas. Specific programmes are necessary with a vision to develop the discipline of Adult /Continuing Education and Extension in the University. One of the thrust areas as per the Guideline is 'Extension and Field Outreach'. The following programmes and activities are focused.

- Continuing education programmes at the grassroot level through the CECs of the NLM and through the National Institute of Open School and State Open Schools
- Communal harmony and peace education
- Human rights and rights of vulnerable groups
- Environmental issues

- Panchayaths and development issues
- Health education for the community and through the Health Care Centre of the University.
- Women's empowerment and
- Social issues and gender issues

The major target groups for the X plan covers, students, non-entrants into university system, women, SC/ST, disadvantaged groups, street children, bonded labour, child workers, Neo-literates, Learners of Continuing Education programme (NLM), out of school youth and senior citizens.

The important programmees and activities include: Development of the discipline (Andragogy/Adult and Continuing Education), Vocational career-oriented programmes, Academic programmes, Leadership and HRD., Quality of Life Improvement Programmes. Individual Interest Promotion Programmes, Social and Citizenship role Awareness Programmes, Resource Support Programmes, Equivalency Programmes etc. Students involved in these programmes should be considered for academic credit in addition to or as a part of their course of studies.

Understanding the Concept of Extension

According to the perception of the UGC, extension is not merely a welfare activity for the deprived social groups; it is a means for making higher education relevant to the needs of the society. It is to be designed as a solution to the existing problems to reduce the gap between the community and higher education.

It is expected to establish a strong and meaningful linkage between the two. It is not simply a process of the higher education institutions moving to the community, with its resources and services, but also an idea of taking the community to the higher education system in the country. As a result of extension process, the student, the teacher, the system (educational institutions, for instance) and the community are equally benefited and enriched. It helps them in the following ways (and it is matter of learning exchange):

1. Enlarging the socio-cultural perspectives of students as well as teachers.
2. Providing first-hand direct experience on social realities which is not available to them within the system.
3. Developing better linkages between institution and community through services and dissemination of information.
4. Bringing about changes in the socio-economic and cultural life of the people in the area (skills and changes in the attitude of the community).
5. Identifying talents and skills available on the campus as well as in the community and meaningfully mobilizing them for developmental activities.
6. Promoting better possibilities of linking extension with curricular activities. The UGC and the government system have accepted extension work as a basis for the career advancement of college/ university teachers.
7. Organise academic programmes to develop the discipline.

EXTENSION: Different Models

Different models in terms of approach and methodology, can be seen in the field of extension in India. Some prominent models include:

1. Institutional Model

In the present system there is a specified model of extension, which is structurally institutionalized. Agricultural universities are examples for institutionalized model of extension. Departments/Centres of Adult and Continuing Education and Extension are also part of the institutional model of extension.

2. *Extension as Part of Curriculum*

In this model, extension will be one of the components in the approved curriculum. For instance, M.Sc. (Home Science) is an academic programme usually offered only in women's colleges. Students have to study number of papers for this Masters programme in which extension is included as a chapter. They are expected to carry out extension programmes or activities as part of their academic programme under the supervision and guidance of teachers.

3. *Extension Linkage Model*

According to this model, extension may not be a part of the curriculum, but indirect linkages are manifest. Extension is not taught as a subject instead, some related activities are carried out. The students, usually at the post-graduate level, may take up some projects or research as part of their practicals or field placement. In the end of the academic programme, in some cases, students will have to submit a research report which forms the part of the evaluation (examination) system. In other words, some linkages are established between the educational system and the society. These linkages will help the students to understand the social realities around him in a better way.

4. *Service/Participant Level*

The educational system offers a number of opportunities for students to participate in extension activities. These opportunities, namely, the National Service Scheme (NSS), National Cadet Corps (NCC) Adult and Continuing Education, and variety of such programmes—will help them gain better experience in their academic life. Though these programmes are not part of the syllabus they are seen as part of the college or institution programme. Both students and teachers are involved in such activities. However, their area of operation is limited. Social surveys, construction of roads, blood donation, free tuition for school children and similar forms of field-oriented programmes/activities are usually done under this programme. Student participation in such programmes is not compulsory but optional. The involvement of students in such productive activities helps them in many ways: developing leadership qualities and values namely, understanding, co-operation, feeling of responsibility, etc. The community also, in turn, benefits from this.

Let us now consider the programmes where extension is made a part of the curriculum:

1. Field interaction is an integral part of the programme.
2. Not less than 20-25 per cent of the curricular time is devoted to community work.
3. Research studies are made with special reference to the field level problems.
4. Community is also involved in the process. Students and teachers absorb the 'participant' culture instead of the traditional 'service' culture.
5. The local self governments are also undergoing changes in their roles and adjusting themselves to accept the changing cultural scenario. They welcome such institutions to be a part of their developmental process.

In these programmes, student participation is graded and credits are given for the work done by them. Centres/ Departments of Adult, Continuing Education and Extension, and Academic Staff Colleges in the university system can give leadership to broaden the extension programmes.

Some of the important activities which promote extension in the present system (in non-agriculture universities and colleges) are:

1. Extension of knowledge resources and manpower resources (through adult, continuing education, population education, legal literacy, environmental education and by offering academic programmes (Post-Graduate Diploma, Post-Graduate Degree, M.Phil., Ph.D. etc.)

2. Transfer of technology and social services (supported by technical institutions, engineering and medical institutions and other institutions of higher education).
3. The concept of 'Community Polytechnic' is popular in technical education. They can support the community with their technical knowhow.
4. Research and Development Programme to strengthen extension and field outreach.
5. Support to SRC/SLMA Programmes (NLM) on continuing education with technical knowhow manpower resources and infrastructure facilities.
6. Consultancy services and support to Local Self Governments, SHGs, NGOs etc.

Some of the major problems/issues seen in the conventional formal system of education (related extension programmes) include:

1. The social commitment of the student, the teacher and the institution is not properly evaluated and recognised.
2. Even though commissions and committees on higher education have stressed the need for extension, administrative and academic reforms are not scientifically implemented to encourage extension programmes.
3. Lack of conceptual understanding and training.
4. Lack of faith in the programme.
5. Administrative constraints and financial limitations.
6. Problems in co-ordination, monitoring, evaluation and documentation.

The following suggestions are given to strengthen Extension as a third dimension in the system.

1. Relevant administrative and academic reforms are necessary to strengthen extension and field outreach.

2. Include extension as part of curriculum, wherever possible.
3. Faculty/discipline may take steps to organise extension programmes and learn from the community.
4. Students, teachers and institutions involved in the programme are to be encouraged and recognised.
5. Co-ordination, monitoring, evaluation and documentation may be made more scientific and systematic.
6. Workshops, seminars and training programmes may be organised to strengthen the students, teachers and heads of institutions.
7. Research related to extension in all disciplines may be encouraged.
8. Establish linkages with industrial, financial and commercial institutions, Governmental organisations and Non-Governmental Organisations, for qualitative and fruitful organisation of the programmes.
9. If necessary, separate organisations can be registered (under Societies Registration Act) to promote extension at the institutional level in order to establish linkages and effective organisation.
10. Extension is a process through which we learn from society and we modify our programmes and activities according to the needs and necessities of the society.
11. Publicity to be given on need and importance of extension through mass media.
12. In brief, extension activities need to be multi-disciplinary in approach and the goal must be development of the individual and society.
13. Extension is to be seen as a process of mutual understanding and development (between academic institutions and the society).

14. Innovative strategies are important Research and development component is necessary for advancement
15. Ensure community participation in all aspects of decision-making
16. A better understanding of community needs and problems
17. Built in monitoring and evaluation system

The institutions interested in extension programmes will have to take steps to ensure the smooth, fruitful and scientific organisation of the programmes. They have to equip themselves better in matters relating to theory and practice of extension, by participating in workshops/seminars to clarify the concepts, ideas and plans of action.

In brief, a practical strategy for extension and field outreach can be summarised in the following way:

Go to the people
Live among them.
Love them
Learn from them
Plan with them
Start with what they know
Build on what they have
Then the people will say:
"We have done it"

Appendix

The National Policy on Education (1986)

Goals

01. Emphasis on socio-economic well-being, competence and creativity of the individual.
02. Development of knowledge and skills in various areas.
03. Development of knowledge and skills for employment opportunities.
04. Integration of the individual in the social system.
05. Development of value-sense of right and wrong.
06. Ensuring equality of educational opportunity to benefit the weaker sections of society.
07. Development of spirit of adventure and mass participation in various programmes.
08. Promotion of integrated as holistic packages of formal and non-formal learning.

REFERENCES

1. UGC, (2004) New Delhi: *Tenth Plan UGC Guidelines on Adult,Continuing Education Extension & Field Outreach.*

2. National Literacy Mission (1999) New Delhi: *An Encyclopedia of Indian Adult Education.*

3. Directorate of Adult Education, Govt. of India, New Delhi (1998) *Outreach.*

4. Directorate of Adult Education, Govt. of India, New Delhi (1989) *A Source Book on Adult Education.*

17

Extension as Third Dimension of the University

Present Status, Problems and Future Directions

D. Uma Devi
P. Adinarayana Reddy

Education is envisaged as an instrument of social transformation. Universities are expected to perform an important role in promoting social change, if they are to retain their legitimacy and gain public support. They need to facilitate the development of capabilities of community for the overall development of the nation and help people to improve the quality of life. Social development of people needs organic linkages between education and society. But at the other end of the spectrum, still there are large number of masses of people are lagged behind with the tangible benefits of the educational system. Still it becomes inaccessible to them. Hence, our education system and its human resource development activities need to focus an appropriate programmes for the total population related to the socio-economic development of the country. This will facilitate the linking of higher education with the development process, conforming to the UGC policy of considering extension as third dimension of higher education which is a need-based, flexible and catering to a large number of people with diverse needs in the society.

In 1960s itself, the Kothari Commission first articulated the concept of extension and the Trinity of Teaching, Research and Extension. The commission stated that the extension was essential for:

— Making education relevant to real life situations.

— For preventing the alienation of the educand from society.

— For developing a sense of responsibility towards society among the educand.

— For deepening the teachers' knowledge through a wider exposure to real life situations.

UGC accepted extension as the third dimension, equal in status with teaching and research, in its landmark policy frame declared in 1977 to benefit both the community and the higher education system.

Extension as the third dimension is an umbrella term which includes adult education, continuing education, population education and community education through field outreach activities. This third dimension aims to promote a meaningful and sustained rapport between the universities and the community. From the beginning, the UGC has emphasized the area based community approach. Community education as a programme as well as approach is intended to help sustain the linkage with all sectors of the community, consisting of all age groups. It is important to adopt an integrated approach of treating the community as a composite social structure in which all its segments complement each other. It aims firstly, to extend knowledge and other institutional resources to the community and secondly, to gain insights from contacts between knowledge, resources and socio-cultural realities with a view to reflecting these in the entire curricular system of higher education including teaching and research. It is a two way process between the experts and the people, an intellectual intervention in the community's living problems which need to be overcome through an educational process. It is that education which helps students to face life and its challenges and creates an ambience for a learning society.

As a part of accepting the extension as third dimension, almost all the universities have established departments/centers of Adult, Continuing Education and Extension to take up the extension activities. The motto behind the establishment of the departments is to eradicate illiteracy, to take up population education, rural development programmes etc., and the colleges and universities are by and large confined to adult literacy and community education, the experience that gained promises great potentialities in developing the entire gamut of non-formal education touching every aspect of the life of common people particularly the needy and weaker sections. But the concept of acceptance of extension as third dimension equal in status with teaching and research was in the context of a growing realization that the universities and colleges having institutional resources—knowledge, manpower and physical-have an obligation to develop sensitivities to involve the development of the community with particular reference to the overall and diverse learning needs of all the segments of the people of the community.

Hence, for the present situation of globalization, privatization and urbanization, the departments recognized that the necessity to change the programmes and their curriculum according to the needs of the society. Now-a-days the departments are planning to conduct both the short-term and long term courses which are vocational based courses ranging from 3 months to 1 year duration as per the needs of the society. Further, they need to change and re-structure their curriculum as per the present needs and in the way of creating employability and enhance the skills and abilities of employability among the people.

Problems

1. Though the UGC has recognized the extension as third dimension of the universities to cater to the needs of the community, majority of the teachers in the universities and colleges have treated these progrmmes as extra curricular activities.
2. There is a lack of co-operation, co-ordination with various agencies engaged in this programme.
3. Training programmes to the functionaries are not need-based and sufficient.

4. Lack of adequate funds to organize the programmes.
5. Lack of adequate monitoring over the programmes.
6. Lack of adequate manpower affecting the implementation of the extension activities.
7. Lack of adequate equipment, transportation for organizing the programmes.
8. Lack of motivation among the community and its participation in the programmes.

Suggestions

1. Changes in the economic environment include the shifting nature of the formal sector in light of global economy, which can provide opportunities for women and men both to balance the family, social and economic responsibilities.
2. The same applies to the growth in inflexibility in the economy, which can provide opportunities for women and men better to balance the family, social and economic responsibilities.
3. Environmental degradation has affected the people, particularly in the rural areas in adverse ways. Majority of the people in rural and remote areas who were dependent on nature for their daily subsistence are finding it increasingly difficult to survive with the resources at their disposal and the demands on their time and energy. Hence, effective eco-management steps to be taken while framing the policies and the universities should play an important role in educating the people particularly, the rural for effective eco-management.
4. The call for gender-sensitive approach should be emphasized by the universities to enable the women and men to recognize and revalue women's experiences, skills and contributions to the economy and social life; to share domestic and caring responsibilities; to participate in the society as

conscious, active and responsible citizen; to enjoy gender relations based on equality and solidarity and to value tolerance, diversity and peaceful resolution of conflict. Policies should be strengthened to make access to the quality education and vocational skills for the women.

5. Educational policies should identify the need for legislation, administrative actions, educational inputs, the media participation and partnerships and resources.
6. Extensive researches must be encouraged and promoted to identify the field level problems and to develop appropriate strategies to overcome the problems.
7. Extension activities should be invited from all the faculties so as to reach the new innovations and facilities to the common man.
8. The extension activities should be innovative approach to cater to the needs of the community. The universities should take necessary steps to strengthen the extension activities and encourage the researchers to carry out the research works.
9. NSS and NCC should be made compulsory to all the students from the beginning of education so as to make them aware about their surroundings and society.
10. The syllabus relating to the community, culture should be incorporated at all levels of educational system in all the faculties.
11. New strategies and approaches should be framed based on the needs of the community particularly the women who need empowerment and the universities should play prominent role in re-structuring its syllabus, administrative procedures, extension activities to achieve the target.

18

The Third Dimension of Universities

Problems And Prospects

D. Janardhana Reddy

The rapid explosion of knowledge that is taking place all over the world created a moral obligation on University system to work for its dissemination in masses, in addition to its age-long work of generating new knowledge. Both are so inherently linked that any inequilibrium between the two will defeat the very purpose of education at all levels. This makes it Emperative for universities to work for promotion of extensive. Hence, the UGC has taken a big step in 1977 and declared extension as the third dimension of Universities, in addition to earlier two-fold dimensions of teaching and research. In fact, extension enriches teaching, learning and research. As a two way process, extension benefits both the academics and community. The All India Conference of Vice-Chancellors of Indian Universities held in 1981 and 1984 have also endorsed the idea of UGC and emphasised that extension should be an integral part of University system. It is heartening to note that in response to UGC's declaration, many universities have not established the Departments of Adult, Continuing Education and Extension.

Problems

It is but natural that any programme will have some inherent problems. The extension programme of Universities is not an exception. In fact it has more problems and most of them remain unresolved.

Though the Universities have accepted and appreciated the concept of extension in principle, the same is not reflected in action. The number of universities participating in adult, continuing education and extension has drastically come down by about 50 per cent. This may be due to universities failure to get the concurrence of the State Government or to accommodate the Departments in their regular budget.

1. Institutionalisation of Extension

In spite of clear declaration by the UGC and the endorsement by the All India Conference of Vice-Chancellors, many Universities have not recognised extension on par with teaching and research and it remains a marginal activity undertaken by the Departments of Adult and Continuing Education. The extension work in universities is confined to a few departments, particularly adult education and it is treated as a UGC funded programme without any allocation from University funds. This lead to discontinuation of extension in the absence of UGC funds. Continuity is essential for extension work. It is necessary that Universities should encourage all Departments to participate in extension work by integrating it in University system and developing an extension culture. The Departments of Adult Education have a greater responsibility in promoting institutionalisation process in all subjects. Adult Education Department is not intended to function as an island by itself but as an agency to foster the process of extension as an integral and inherent part of the academic life of teachers and students in all departments. Appropriate evaluation methods should also be devised for assessment of this work. A beginning may be made by providing at least 25 per cent time allocation for extension work in all Departments. Similarly, the University has to first assess what they can extend to the society and identify extendable resources and develop mechanism to extend the support.

2. Resource Mobilisation and Coordination

Enormous amounts of resources are available in various Government Departments for the purpose of Information, Extension and Communication (IEC) evaluation and research activities. For instance, National/State Aids Control Organisation provides funds for awareness generation, Ministry of Tribal Welfare for research, CAPART for creation of scientific temper etc. There are many funding agencies in the country to support extension activities. The services of lions club, rotary clubs and other voluntary agencies can be utilised by proper coordination. Corporate sector is also spending a portion of their profit for social service. Similarly, the banking sector has a specific allocation of money for social service activities. The universities have trained manpower to take up research and evaluation projects. At present there is a lack of coordination and collaboration at the state and the district level with various agencies involved in developmental programmes, including adult education programme of the Government. It is sadening to note that there is no effective coordination with other departments even within University system. Though adult education and NSS are community service activities, adequate coordination between the two is lacking. It is high time for University Departments of Adult Education to establish effective linkages and networking with Governmental and Non-Governmental organisations. This would solve the problem of resource crunch and facilitate continuation of extension work even in the absence of UGC funds.

3. Professionalism

About two decades ago, the Professor Ramlal Parikh's Committee, constituted in 1986 to review the UGC programme of Adult, Continuing Education and Extension, has observed that a large number of persons working in the Departments of Adult Education have no specialisation in adult education and extension. Professor Shah, in his paper on empowerment of weaker sections through University Extension Programmes, has opined that one of the reasons for the ineffectiveness of extension programmes may be due to the lack of professional expertise in the area of extension among the existing staff members of the Departments of Adult Education. He said that a survey of the educational background of the staff members of the Departments of Adult Education revealed that a hardly 10 per cent of them have specialisation in extension at Masters and Doctorate level. The majority of them have the background of humanities, social sciences and other science subjects. This might be the reason for the lack of development of innovative models of extension.

In view of the above, the professional competence of adult education staff in the Universities needs to be improved considerably (Ramlal Parikh Committee). The staff should be motivated to do P.G. Dipoma in Adult and Continuing Education. It is also necessary to insist upon adult education staff to attend adult education refresher courses organised by the academic staff college for the purpose of promotion under career advancement scheme (CAS). It is unfortunate to note that some academic staff colleges are unable to run the adult education refresher courses due to insufficient number of takers. They attended refresher courses of other disciplines. This practice may be stopped. In addition, Universities may be encouraged to start P.G. Diploma course in Adult Education and Extension Education through distance mode. Similarly, one of the Universities in each state or zone may be recognised as a resource centre for conducting training programmes. Adult education may also be included in the cultural exchange programme of the UGC.

4. Promotion of Research

Though there is a significant growth in research work in the field of adult education in the last three decades, it does not commensurate with the University Department of Adult Education and the size of the staff. There are not many scholarly publications in adult education and extension work. Adult education cannot grow as a discipline and it can not be implemented effectively, unless it is supported by research studies. There is need to encourage both basic research and action research by the adult education faculty. It has been observed that while some of the departments have done excellent extension work, there is no documentation on their work. It may be due to attitudinal problem or a skill problem. There is also need to start professional journal of adult education and to encourage the faculty members to contribute study-based quality articles. As stated earliest adult education faculty have different educational backgrounds it is necessary that they should be trained in social science research methodology to provide necessary skills and to enable them to conduct many research studies. Teacher fellowships as well as Doctoral and Post-doctoral fellowships should be instituted in the Departments of Adult Education where there are facilities for M.Phil and Ph.D programmes.

5. Extension Work and CAS

There is a provision in the guidelines on career advancement scheme (CAS) and also the guidelines for the recruitment of staff in the departments of Adult Education to give weightage to extension work. It is observed that no weightage is given for extension work. This may be one of the reasons for the neglect of extension work in other departments of the University. Extension work should be given due weightage at the time of promotions under CAS. There is also a need to develop appropriate evaluation mechanism to assess extension work quantitatively and qualitatively. Similarly, publications in extension should also be given the weightage. This step will enhance participation of faculty members of other disciplines in extension work.

Conclusion

The UGC has highlighted the significance of extension in several policy documents, especially after the formulation of Policy Framework of Higher Education (1977) which recognised extension as the third dimension of universities in addition to teaching and research. Though some progress has been made in this direction, there are many miles to go. Effective measures have to be taken at different levels—UGC, University and the Departments of Adult Education—to ensure higher participation of teachers and students of all disciplines. Some of the measures which need immediate attention of appropriate bodies are:

1. Institutionalisation of extension in university system and its incorporation in the curriculum of all disciplines by the University;

2. Effective coordination and collaboration with governmental and non-governmental organisations to mobilise resources by the Department of Adult Education;
3. Promotion of professional competence among adult education staff through academic courses and refresher courses by the UGC and University;
4. Promotion of research in extension through M.Phil and Ph.D, research projects and publications by the Department of Adult Education and University; and
5. Insisting upon contribution to extension service at the time of promotion under CAS by the UGC and University.

19

Revamping the Field Outreach and Extension Activities for the Universities through Students Community

A Model

Naseem Akthar
K.K. Palani

Introduction

Universities should involve the field outreach activities with the coordination and co-operation of the other Departments of the University including the Students and the Teachers. This can be achieved through the active involvement of the students community for the outreach activities. To bring about the changes in the selected underprivileged society in the aspects of Literacy, Continuing Education, Health, Empowerment and Emancipation, Self Help Group, Knowledge in community colleges, Entrepreneurship, Legal literacy and Consumer Education etc., through the University field outreach and extension activities.

Objectives of the Programme

To make the students to have the social responsibilities over the society and sensitize the students about the under privileged people living in the society. To bring about the attitudinal changes among the Students as well as under privileged people through the involvement of the field outreach and extension activities through students community. To liberate the minds of men and women from harmful tradition, conservatism, prejudices, superstition and help them to have better understanding of social, economical and political life by involving both of them in the Field outreach and extension activities of the Universities.

Collaborating Bodies

The collaborative bodies of this programme are State Resource Centre for Non-formal Education, Department of Health and Family Welfare, Tamil Nadu Social Welfare Board, Women Development Corporation. Slum Clearance Board and Aids prevention and Control Society etc. They also support us by providing their centres like corporation Schools, Valwadies, Anganwadies, Community Centres and Continuing Education Centres as our resource centres. The State Resource Centre support the programme in providing training and teaching learning materials for the teachers, students, animators and community people. Women Development Corporation will provide training for organising self help group and entrepreneurship development programme for women. Apart from this involving the like-minded organization which were working in the slums nearby the Universities with similar concern (i.e.) NGOs' Training Institute, Youth clubs, local associations and Exnora International etc. those source will be very useful for the community based programme.

Responsibility of the Staff

1. Co-ordinator
2. Programme/Field staff

The co-ordinator will be incharge of the whole programme. The programme/Field staff will be assist the students and the community.

Training and Orientation

Each Department Students will be given two hours orientation by the coordinator prior to their exposure visit. In the first level the students will be briefed about the programmes, and about the nature of work. In the Second level of the training the students will be emphasized about the need, the method and the purpose of carrying out community activities. Students training will be held simultaneously. Every year 3 to 4 training programmes to students will be organized to strengthen their knowledge about the community activities. Need based staff-in-charge training programme also will be conducted.

Shaping the Department into a Team

After the orientation and training programme the students will be split into teams to the different sectors of work. Each team will comprise of 10-15 students who will work under a group representative. Students would be free to choose their team, with the guidance of their respective department staff incharge and according to their area of interest. The team will consist of:

- Non-formal teaching team
- Health and Hygiene team
- Women Empowerment team
- Youth Development team
- Regular and Evening teaching team
- Continuing Education team Literacy team
- Socio-Cultural team and so on

The team leader is the representative of the group. He/she will also coordinate the team activities. All the team members will combine together for the common activity of the department. As such all the Departments will come together for the common activities of the outreach/activities.

Exposure Visit

Students will be taken to the field for exposure. They will be introduced to the community. The work hours of the outreach activity would begin from the day of the exposure visit.

Role of Students in Outreach Activity

Outreach activity is considered as an important aspects in 9th and 10th plan period of UGC. Hence, the outreach activity is a compulsory programme for all the I-year and II year post-graduates students of the University Department. All these students will undergo a fieldwork in a selected area of their interest. Each department will work for 1 day in a week. Students are free to work in the field during the outreach activity. Students has to report to the co-ordinator and concerned staff. The students who fail to complete their minimum requirement will be given opportunities to compensate the outreach activity.

Monitoring and Evaluation

Each student has to submit the report about the activities performed in the field, based on the report the group report will be prepared and each group report of the Department would be consolidated. This has to be kept as a document of the work. Outreach programme has to be celebrated in the University every year. Feedback would be collected from the community teachers, students, Community volunteers and the community people.

20

Extension as Third Dimension in the Universities

Present Status, Problems and Future Directions

P. Syama Thrimurthy

The Impact of Globalisation has placed new demands on the Education System. Transformation with rapid change is taking place everywhere. Students and youth have to be prepared by the university to adopt change and learn new skills in accordance with the new demand of the World of Work. In other words, university has to prepare the students to be LIFE LONG LEANERS. Only then will the student be able to sustain his knowledge and skills at the national and international level. On one hand they have to enhance students employability skills through formal systems, on the other hand through the non-formal system attempts are being made for giving education to the unreached. In this process, Universities are trying to integrate formal and non-formal education by opening their doors to adult leaner for Life-long Learning Programmes and by making the university.

Adult Learner-Friendly Institution

It is here that all the Departments in the University especially Adult Education Department that has to play a more dynamic and pro-active role. It is to move from the periphery to the center stage of the university system. Simultaneously, developing human resource expertise in the subject of Adult, Continuing Education, Extension and Field Outreach. Along with Teaching and Research University Grants Commission has accepted and recognized Extension as the Third Dimension of the University. It had been giving directions from time to time to re-orient the universities for fulfilling the third dimension. Extension activities facilitate to bring the University and the Community closer. Universities and Colleges can no longer remain as knowledge centers, they need to establish rapport with the society for which they have to move out of the university and reach out to different places sharing their acquired knowledge, resources and manpower. This was emphasized in the Ninth Plan Period and in fact has facilitated the Adult Education Departments to cast their own Plan of Action for Extension being specific to their own university.

Acharya Nagarjuna University is a rural University with more than 300 affiliated colleges spread out in the three districts namely, Krishna, Guntur and Prakasam. Department of Adult Continuing Education is one among the 37 Departments in the university. Department is fully engaged in conducting Extension activities in addition to research. During the Tenth Plan period the Department had conducted Three months Certificate Course in the years 2003-04 and 2004-05 simultaneously in two centers in two districts. Five Days certificate courses for the rural women, especially for SC, ST and BC women were also conducted. Over and above that the Department had conducted more than twenty-nine extension activities till today. These programmes were organized at school level, college level, University level and at the community level.

School Level

- Legal Metrology
- Fire Accidents-Causes, Prevention and Extinction of Fire
- Dental Camps in Govt. and Private Schools
- Essay writing Competitions on:
  - World Population Day
  - International Literacy Day
  - Disabled Day

College Level

- Women's Rights
- Certificate course for promoting women entrepreneurship
- Income generating and Individual Interest Programme
- Awareness Programmes on How to improve psychological beauty
- Women Entrepreneurship programme
- Awareness on cosmetology and skin care
- Tapping the talents of the untouched
- Demonstration of Beauty Culture and Health Care
- Organisation of:
  - — World Population Day
  - — International Literacy Day
  - — World AIDS Day
  - — Disabled Day
  - — Women's Day
- Elocution, Essay writing and debate Competition on:
  - — World Population Day
  - — International Literacy Day
  - — World AIDS Day
  - — Disabled Day

University Level

- Haemophilia
- Food Additives
- Food Adulteration
- Mega Health Camps
- Consumer Protection
- Communication Skills

- Soya Bean—A nutritive Supplement
- Symposium on Women Empowerment
- How to overcome Psychological Problems
- Student's Workshop on Fieldwork Practicum
- Requirements - Identification for a Public Enterprise
- Programmes on STRESS Management (every year)
- Awareness Programmes on the Educational facilities to the Disabled

Community Level

- Aharamu-Arogyamu
- Certificate Courses for the women
- Skin Care Programme for youth
- Programme for the Senior Citizens on Yoga and Accupressure
- Stress Management Programme for the housewives
- Identification of diseases in Flower, Fruit and Vegetable farming—Programme for the farmers

Issues And Problems and Future Directions in Conducting Extension Activities

Department of Adult, Continuing education, Extension and Field Outreach of Acharya Nagarjuna University is aggressively working in the direction of the Third Dimension, i.e Extension. Our experience helps us to spell out some of the issues and problems that we generally encounter which are presented below.

Conceptual Understanding of the Functioning of the Department of Adult Education

The functioning of the Department of Adult Education has been changing from Plan to Plan as per UGC direction. Simultaneously there is a need to change in the thinking process of the authorities of the universities. Extension activities can be conducted only when there is motivation, encouragement and co-operation from the authorities. Positive approach of the authorities to the functioning of the Department will always help to achieve the objectives. Hence administrators have to be involved in conducting the extension activities. The more they are involved it facilitates both the organizers and the university to come out with expected results.

Coordination of Men, Material and Money

In conducting Extension activities men, material and money are the basic requirements. Coordination of these three is an essential factor for the success of the Extension activities. As the activities are for different target groups and for different sections of the community, good public relations has to be developed and maintained. Organisers always have to be alert with watchful eyes looking out for good resourceful persons for making the Extension activity meaningful and useful to the target group. Relevant material required for conducting the programmes varies from programme to programme hence, collecting the materials like booklets, pamphlets, relevant literature, posters, handouts, audio-video matrerial etc in advance and presenting it on time is another important aspect. At every step there is a financial need. Budget planning, implementation and accounting the expenditure is a tedious, time consuming and risk involved task for the organizers.

Extensive Travelling

Extension activities are conducted at various levels and to the different sections of the society and in far of places. This involves travelling to far of places and to remote corners from the university. Travelling is no doubt exciting but extensive travelling under hectic time pressure is not an easy task. An exclusive vehicle is a basic requirement for the University Adult Education Departments for conducting Extension activities.

Time Schedule

Planning, maintenance and sticking to the time schedule is a very important aspect while conducting Extension activities. Planning for the programme is done quite in advance, the time schedules are informed quite in advance, in spite of that the Resources persons and guests turn up late hence the programme gets delayed and consequently leading to a delay in all the successive events. Organizers have to compromise or rather adjust to with the existing situation. At times it is beyond their control. At times the beneficiaries patience is being tested and the organizers have to adopt to different techniques to engage the target groups.

Freedom to the Organisers

Department can spear ahead with the Extension Activities provided they are free from the administrative procedures.

Matching Minds

Extension activities are always cheerful, meaningful and fruitful only when the organizers share the spirit of responsibility and work with the team spirit. Only when the thoughts and actions match the activities will be successful, hence matching minds is very essential for conducting and continuing extension activities. Extension activities looks for people who have igniting minds and who have spark for such kind of activities.

Timely Financing by the UGC and University

Conducting Extension Activities should be a continuous process to establish rapport between the universities and the community. These activities are linked with grants from the UGC. The timely release of grants for the Plan periods will facilitate to continue the Third Dimension of EXTENSION.

Future Direction

The end result of Extension activity is always fruitful, but prior to that the amount of exertion involved in implementing the activities is unaccounted. Motivation, Co-operation and encouragement from the authorities, beneficiaries will always boost up the spirits of the organizers. Only then the UGC's goal to transform the University system into an active instrument of social change through the institutionalisation of Extension as the third dimension can be ensured and make the system *adult learner-friendly and pro-lifelong learning*.

21

Globalization and Community Problems

Emerging Role of Universities

H.M. Panchaksharaiah

The present chapter examines the extension role of Universities and Problems and future expectations. Universities are not ivory towers. Education, particularly higher education, is envisaged as an instrument of social transformation. Universities are therefore expected to perform an important role in promoting social change. The "Kothari Commission" clearly established the need for linkage between University and Society. Rightly UGC has accepted extension as the third dimension of the University. The other two dimensions being are teaching and research. The University or the college in primarily a reflection of the society in which it exit. If universities fail to recognise the needs of the society, all the efforts of the higher education are wasted. Not only dissemination of knowledge but understanding the problems of the community and developing the appropriate intervention of the Universities is very much needed.

In India there are more than 350 Universities and 13000 colleges which covers hardly more than 7 per cent of the hundred million nation. In terms of plan allocation to higher education and the rich human resources that is contained in Universities is not properly utilised. In the present era of globalisation, privatization and liberalisation in Indian societies the role of Universities has become all the more critical. The process of globalisation will critically affect already marginalised groups that more people may be marginalised social inequalities may be further increased. To equip the Indian society to face the new challenges of globalization. The Universities have to take more serious role as an intervention institution in the path of social development. Before University can transfer society it must be transformed from within. Administratives, Alumin, State Legislatives, faculty, Private supporters and students must realise and accept that the function of higher education should be a solution to societial problems. The University needs to stand unique as an institution devoted to solving urgent societal problems. University can play the role of a catalyst in social development. Some of the functions that the Universities can take up is as follows:

1. Education of people at the undergraduate and graduate levels for citizenship roles.
2. Equipping people for successful careers.
3. Conducting research on a variety of problems.
4. Promoting cultivation of the arts.
5. Preserving the freedom of intellectual pursuit.
6. Providing specialised service on needs outside the University.
7. Taking the lead in solving problem vital to survival.
8. Providing outreach educational opportunities through community service or extension programmes.

Even in the most developed countries like USA, Universities have incorporated the extension as a critical dimension of the Universities. Universities develop the programme, curriculum and research on the basis of community one scholar has even suggested that universities be renamed as "communiversities" where community needs and problem are central focal points for University activities. Universities should overcome the 'leninst' slogan'. To study, to study and once again to study. By passing concentration on elitist teaching may release equal partnership, energies, synergetic effects in solutions of social problems.

In most of the Universities and Colleges in India, the outreach activities are in the form of extension services is limited only to NSS and other limited services. The role of University as a change agent, a facilitator is absent in most of the Indian Universities. In Japan Universities and research organisations were greatly involved in industrial development by support in cause of small scale industries. Japan emerged as a strong contendor to USA mainly because of the nature and type of the research that was carried in Japanese Universities. Rather than focussing on basic research, applied research which is development-oriented a problem solving were taken on priority issues. Contrary in India the Universities have become deadwood in promoting an intended functions especially the third dimension extension.

The teaching function of University and college falls into two aspects.

(a) Preparation of individuals for various careers.

(b) Training of individual teachers.

It is not enough when the students is trained in particular occupation. They should also be equipped with skills, techniques, to promote positive human relationships and capacity to cope with change. For example in Karnataka a large number of medical colleges were have up. The students who graduate from these colleges are not willing to go to the villages to serve. Even the medical colleges, are not playing a crucial role in providing service to the community health problems. Karnataka state also has the distinction of largest number of engineering colleges. Most of the projects that emerge out of the engineering colleges are of decorative nature. When the high school girl could develop a prototype for taking care the problem of toilet disposal in railway stations. Universities and colleges have become a factories producing graduates they are not able to develop thinking analytical constructive socially sensitive personalities. If University graduates are which they live and work, in other words to establish some horizontal relationships within the community, efforts to create a more satisfying life for all residents will be difficult to achieve student in higher education should be given exposure to community theory and education this could be built in the curriculum itself. The teachers should serve in various roles in addition to the classroom teaching. The teaching function should include theoritical and practical related knowledge of the students to create viable links between academic world community to promote better integration of students into society after they complete this education. Habits, increased willingness and ability to interact with community should be made the part of teaching function appropriate value orientations increased mutual trusts among the University teachers, students and community, should be encouraged.

The research function in term of quality and quantity the universities are producing M.Phil's and Ph.D's but their net contribution to social development and problem solving function is negligible. Sometime back in Indian Institute of Management Bangalore, a Professor with lot of social commitment initiated a project to improve bullock cart. India with a hundred million people out of 70 per cent are living in rural area, have engulfed in many problems which require immediate attention. For example, Universities can do a lot of work by assuring support in providing clean drinking water to more than six lakh villages this would have cut down the expenditure on health.

Another important research need is the evolution of on-going community education and other types of developmental programmes. A viable partnership between the community and the other higher education could result in evaluation specialist from local colleges and universities carrying out various evolution efforts on community plans and programmes. Universities have to develop network of NGOs activities, providing technical support and guidance assisting them in taking up a critical developmental programmes. The Universities can take up need-based research in addressing community problems. The consultancy function of the University at present is not satisfactory. The consultancy which is carried out in premier institutions is mostly catering to the needs of affordable big industries. The University can very effectively harness the resources at its disposal, faculty, laboratory, computer centre and instrumentation centre to help the needy in the community to find solutions. Various university personnel interested in human resource development could provide counsel courses and training resources. Adult Education specialist could develop credit or non-credit workshops aimed at upgrading knowledge and skills. Special education experts develop a clinic that serves community residents. Psychology department and social work department have a large role to play in assuring community mental health as well as social development. In a country like India, where large number of rural development programmes are initiated. Programmes are not really reaching the needed beneficiaries due to various reasons. The success of these programmes to a large extent depends on experts from the University participating. The government should also ensure and make a political will to involve universities in its programmes. The government machinery shy away from the university in tapping the vast human resources. In the present scenario, universities should not be confined only as knowledge production centers. "Knowledge is power" the universities can bring about tremendous social transformation through conversion of knowledge to power. The Universities have to emerge as developmental centers, catalyst of social change and primer movers of developmental activities.

New Functions for Extension Service to Consider

There are various new functions related to the community that universities and colleges could take up. More and more universities adapting issues with social relevance as their extension theme. For example, Delhi University has taken up womens empowerment like that the Universities could become region specific issue, specific extension activities. The NSS which is an operation throughout the country through Universities and Colleges. This organiastion can be effectively re-designed, restructured and strengthened.

The exposure in the students to the community problems will sensitise them and help them to have proper mindset. A nationwide awareness campaign regarding various social problems can be achieved, students should be trained with skills, attitudes, values and models which will enable them to act as change agents. The University with its faculty and its students can play a key role in bringing about communal harmony by working with people. Problems like unemployment can be tackled by Universities by developing job-oriented courses. Continuous upgradation redesigning of courses linking higher education to the needs of the society should be the priority agenda for the Universities. In the ninth and tenth plans extensive programmes have been envisaged. In the era of globalization Indian society with its large number of marginalised pockets of social groups are sure to encounter new set of problems. If these problems are not taken care by the Universities, the problems can emerge as sever threats to the social development. Higher education is thrown open with this many foreign players get into the higher education. Those higher education institutions will not be interested in community education. It is our only conventional universities have to tackle this problems. The UGC since last decade is giving more importance and weightage to the extension dimension of the University. The UGC has to further harness the Universities to come out from their conventional role playing to the role of performing meets needed social obligations. The Universities should create and recreate, structure and restructure continuously to cater to the needs of communities in which they exist. Then only universities and higher education can become meaningful.

22

Extension Programmes at Bharathidasan University

Present Status, Problems and Future Directions

K. Parthasarathy
S. Durga

Concept of Extension

Extension is education and its purpose is to change attitudes and practices of people with whom the work is done. Extension is an out-of-school education process. It involves working with people along the lines of their current interest and need which are closely related to gaining livelihood, improving level of living, and catering the needs of community welfare: utilizing particular teaching techniques, conducted with the aid of certain supporting activities and carried on with a distinctive spirit of co-operation, mutual respect, and help.

Objectives of Extension

The essence of extension education is the adoption of changed practices by individuals based on their own decisions, leading to community or groups.

- The extension therefore, is to develop the individuals in the community and improve the well-being of all the rural people within the framework of national, economic, social and political policies and conditions.
- The objective are, in the material side to increase production in educational side to increase knowledge,

to improve strategies of technology skill and help people to change their attitudes from traditional and static to scientific and dynamic and social and cultural sphere, to develop the community through consolidating and strengthening the local groups such as youth clubs, mahila mandals, co-operatives, panchayats, etc.

Extension work of all dimensions will lead to the total development of the community. It may be of:

- Adult Education Programme
- Agricultural Programme
- Women Development Programme
- Child Care and Supplementary Programme
- Entrepreneurship Programme—Small Scale Industries, Health and Nutrition, Hunger Free Programme, Refresher Courses of Short Duration, People Education etc., (Ensminger, 2000).

UGC's Efforts on Extension

The University Grants Commission (UGC), which is the apex body for higher education system in India, in their policy frame of Higher Education, recognized Extension as the third dimension of the institution of Higher Education in addition to the earlier two-fold Dimension of Teaching and Research. Currently there are about 102 Universities having Departments/Centres of Adult, Continuing Education and Extension spread all over the country. The UGC's policy statement 1977, revised guidelines 1982, 1988 and the recent new guidelines 2004 on Adult and Continuing Education underlined the need for extension activities by the Higher Education system. The third Dimension aims to promote a meaningful and sustained rapport between the colleges/ University and the community. Further, the university should absorb the concept of extension culture and efforts should be taken to allot 25 per cent time-period for the off campus, extension work through community education.

Further, the UGC review committee set up under the chairmanship of Dr. Ram Lal Parikh in 1986, had suggested extension activities to be undertaken by the institution of higher education such as universities and colleges and policy-making bodies like the Ministry of Human Resource Development, Government of India. Thus, it becomes a necessity to all those who are involved in education at any level, to understand the need, principles, strategies and techniques of extension education, so that they could develop positive attitude for extension education activities and acquire the skills in communication and techniques of extension education. Extension may also involve closer interaction with the society and could be dovetailed with the programmes of rural development. This should aim at inculcation of scientific temper and awareness of impact of several factors in day-to-day life—proper utilization of the fruit of science and technology, environment, education, legal literacy, national integration etc., among the community around the university.

Keeping these above perspectives in mind, the Bharathidasan University in the State of Tamil Nadu, has established a separate Centre for Adult, Continuing Education and Extension during 1985-86 for looking after the 'Extension' component both at the University and its affiliated colleges levels.

About the Centre for Adult, Continuing Education and Extension [CACEE]

The CACEE is an Academic and Non-Vacation Department established with the financial support of UGC in the year 1985-86. It caters to the "extension" needs of over 95 Arts and Science/Fine Arts/Education Colleges and over 25 Approved Institutions covering seven districts in the central part of Tamil Nadu. The student strength in the affiliated colleges number over 1.3 lakhs. The centre has 10 staff members including temporary project staff. The liability of the staff of the CACEE has been taken over by the Govt. of Tamil Nadu from April 1997 onwards. The CACEE undertakes Teaching, Research, and Extension. Two faculty members of the CACEE were served as

Syndicate Members of the Bharathidasan University. The Director of the CACEE is representing as ex-officio member in the senate and SCAA. Director has served as Dean, Faculty of Arts, Bharathidasan University. Presently the CACEE has occupied a major position in the newly formed School of Education, Bharathidasan University and the Director of CACEE has been appointed as Co-ordinator of the School.

Teaching Programmes

PG in MA Rural Technology (Focusing on Adult & Extension Education), M.Phil., in Adult and Continuing Education (FT/PT/Distance Education), number of Certificate and Diploma Courses offered jointly with Institute for Entrepreneurship and Career Development, Bharathidasan University, Tiruchirappalli. There are functional tie-ups with reputed NGOs, Rural Institutions and .select Development Departments for exposing the field realities to the students. During IXth and Xth plan (up to December 2005), 54 PG students have successfully come out of the course and sixty per cent of them are presently working in NGOs, Research Institutes and Development Departments and drawing monthly salary ranging from Rs. 2,500 to 18,000/-.

Research Programmes

The CACEE is one of the three centres in Indian Universities to have facility for M.Phil and Ph.D in Adult and Continuing Education. The centre has produced 10 Ph.Ds and 5 M.Phils in Adult and Continuing Education. All the Ph.D and M.Phil. holders are well placed. Operationalised number of minor and major research projects on Extension Education and mobilized Rs. 45 lakhs from external funding agencies. Currently three major research projects are being operationalised, which is sponsored by UGC and Ministry of Social Justice and Empowerment, New Delhi with the total grant-in-aid of Rs. 6.40 lakhs. Presently, 11 candidates are pursuing Ph.D programme. It is worthy to note that two scholars have qualified UGC-NET in Adult/Continuing Education and receiving UGC SRF and JRF Fellowships.

Extension Programmes

Past Activities

The CACEE of Bharathidasan University, for the past several years, the following Extension Education Programmes were implemented by the University and its affiliated colleges by involving the students and teachers at the grossroot level.

- Adult Literacy through Centre Based Approach
- Mass Programme for Functional Literacy (Each one Teach One)
- Population Education
- Total Literacy Campaign
- National Service Scheme
- Cultural Activities
- Youth Red Cross Activities
- AIDS Education
- Post-Literacy and Continuing Education
- Self-Employment and Income Generating Programmes
- Organizing number of Capacity Building Programmes etc.

Present Activities

Part-IV in UG Curriculum

CACEE has been instrumental in incorporating the Part-IV Extension as part of DG curriculum. The Part-IV Extension helps the students to widen their knowledge in the field of culture, arts and related activities. Through Part - IV, the students get the chances to work in the specific field and get a field exposure. It also develops communication skills and induces innovative ideas. The subjects like National Service Scheme, National Cadet Corps, Performing Arts, Rotract/Leo Clubs, Environmental Education, First Aid, Health Education and Continuing Education are coming under the Part-IV.

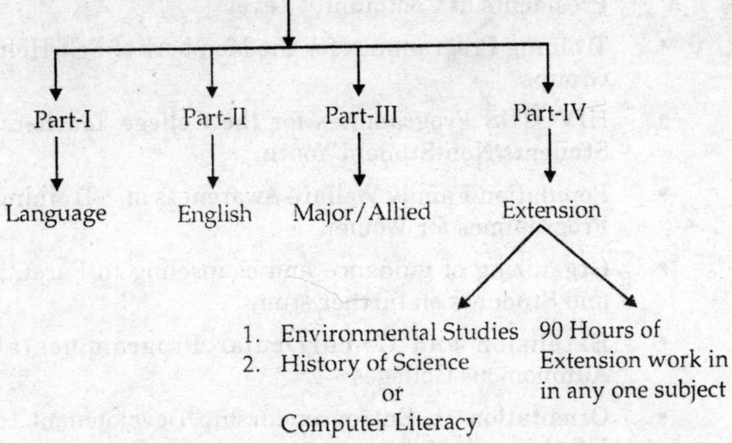

An Advisory Board on Extension (ABE) draws the Extension Activities consecutively two years of the UG courses. The activities are based on Practicals/Field Activities/Extension Activities outside the class hours. The student's minimum participation of 45 hours per year and 90 hours in two years is compulsory. The ABE monitors all the extension activities. The assessment of the Performances /Works/Services are made by the faculty-in-charge and recommends the grades to be awarded by the ABE. Grades are awarded for participation, performances and behaviour of the students like A- Distinction, B- Very Good, C- Good and D- Fair.

Structure of the ABE

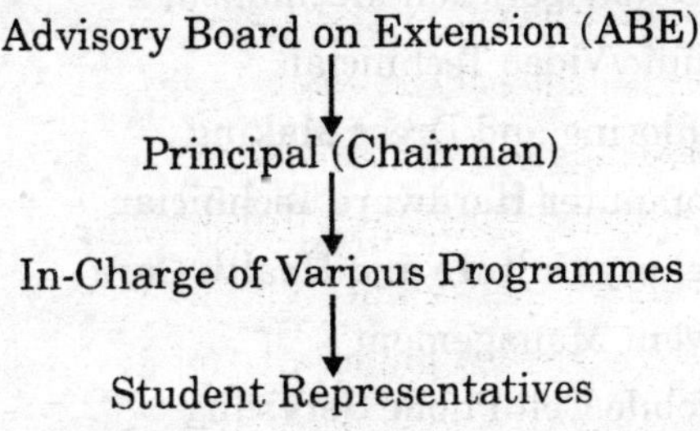

Field Outreach

- Training Programmes for the Women Panchayat Presidents at Community Level
- Training Programmes for the Members of Self-Help Groups
- HIV/AIDS Programmes for the College Teachers/ Students/Non-Student Youth
- Population/Family Welfare Awareness and Training Programmes for Women
- Organizing of guidance and counseling to Parents and Students on further study
- Extension and Co-curricular Programmes at Autonomous Colleges
- Orientation on Entrepreneurship Development to UG/PG students
- Orientation on Extension and Co-curricular Activities to UG Students of Non autonomous colleges

Need Based Short-Term Courses

The following need based short-term continuing education courses, specially designed for SC/ST Women and Out-of-School Youth, are being conducted in order to generate self-employment opportunities.

- Entrepreneurship Development
- Electrical Technician
- UPS and Inverter Manufacture
- AC/Refrigeration Mechanism
- Audio/Video Technician
- Tailoring and Dress Making
- Computer Hardware Technician
- Beauty Culture and Health Care
- Event Management
- Mobile/Cell Phone Servicing
- Bakery Products—Fast Foods

Continuing Education Courses

The following Certificate/Diploma courses are being offered on self-supported basis in collaboration with Institute for Entrepreneurship and Career Development of Bharathidasan University:

- Entrepreneurship Development
- Visual Communication
- Journalism and Mass Communication
- Multimedia and Web Design
- Applied Nutrition
- Public Relations
- Herbal Technology
- Counseling and Guidance
- Human Resources Management
- Computer Hardware
- Industrial Bio-technology
- Bio-informatics
- Computer Applications

Inter-College Campus Recruitment

- Organizing of Inter-Collegiate Campus Interviews for Weaker Sections studying in the colleges.
- Organizing of Inter-Collegiate Campus Interviews for final year UG students.
- Organizing of Inter-Collegiate Campus Interviews for final year PG students.
- Organizing of Inter-Collegiate Campus Interviews for final year students studying through correspondences courses of the university.
- Organizing Inter-Collegiate level programmes on Face the Future
- Organizing of Inter-Collegiate Campus Interviews for previous year students.

Flow Chart of Outreach/Extension Model in Bharathidasan University

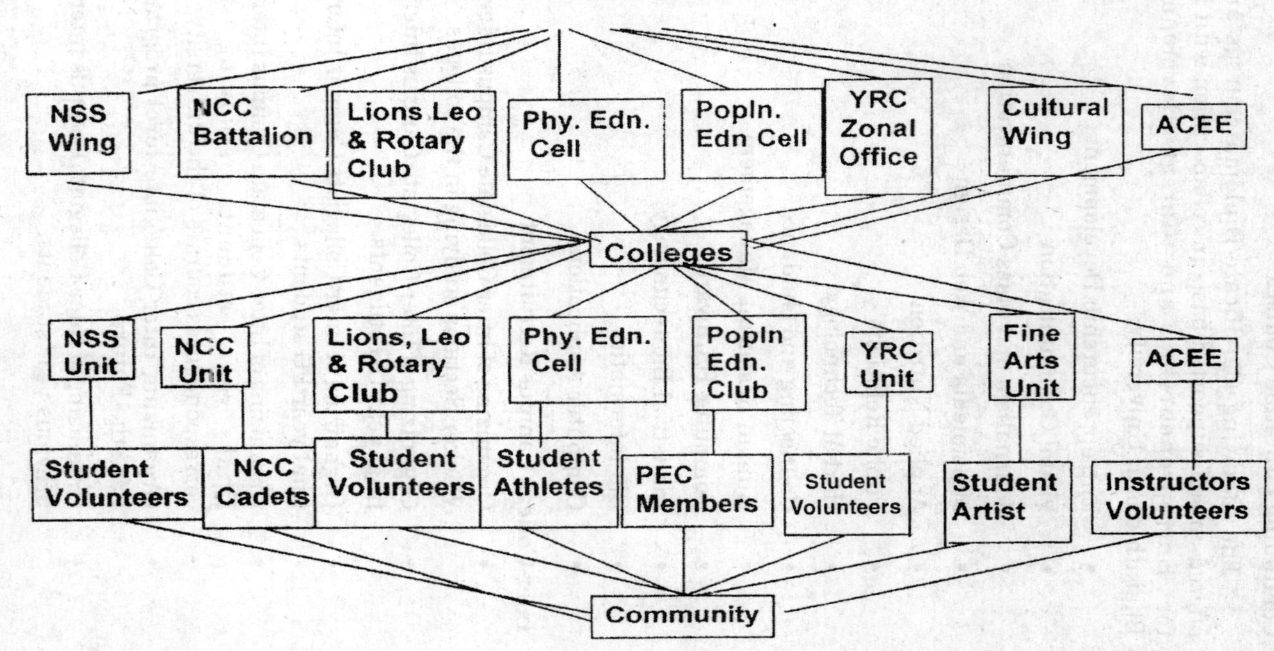

A Few Problems

- Accountability of Staff
- Employability of Students and Trainees
- Inadequate Recognisation of the Extension Works ~ UOC's Funding Policies on Extension Works

Some Future Directions

- Formation of School of Non-Formal Education/Social Engineering—Networking with a few Foreign Universities
- Undertaking multi-disciplinary Research Works
- Concentrating on Entrepreneurship Development Programmes

REFERENCES

1. Bharat J Ethithor, (1996)—*Adult Education and Extension*, A. P. H. Publishing Corporation, New Delhi.
2. CACEE, (2004), *CACEE's Brochure*, Bharathidasan University, Tiruchirappalli-24.
3. Pankajam, G., (2000), *Extension—Third Dimension of Education*, Gyan Publishing House, New Delhi.
4. Parthasarathy, K., (1991), "*A Manual on Implementation of Extension Activities through Students and Teachers of the University and Colleges*" Centre for Adult, Continuing Extension, Bharathidasan University, Tiruchirappalli.
5. Parthasarathy, K., Anadamoorthy, V and Harikumar, V., (Ed), (2003), "*Literacy and Development*" (Vol-I), State Resource Centre for Non-Formal, Adult and Continuing Education (SRC), Chennai and Centre for Adult, Continuing Education and Extension, Bharathidasan University, Tiruchirappalli.
6. Parthasarathy, K., Anadamoorthy, V and Harikumar, V., (Ed), (2004), "*Research on Literacy - Literacy and Development*" (Vol-II), State Resource Centre for Non-Formal, Adult and Continuing Education (SRC), Chennai and Centre for Adult, Continuing Education and Extension, Bharathidasan University, Tiruchirappalli-23.
7. Parthasarathy, K., (2005)-*CACEE News* of Centre for Adult, Continuing Extension, Bharathidasan University, Tiruchirappalli-23.

8. Prabhudass, (1997), - "Extension Activity Models Adopted by Students and Teachers of Autonomous Colleges in Tamil Nadu, India" - (Unpublished dissertation), Centre for Adult, Continuing Extension, Bharathidasan University, Tiruchirappalli-24.

Website Address

www.uge.ac.in

http://www.uge.ac-in/financia/support/intro/.html

http://www.metu-edu.tr/uakasasu/chaos

Index

E

R

S

T

U

❑❑❑